In 1776, Thomas Paine's words
sparked a revolution.
Today, a new revolution of thought begins
right now, with *you.* . . .

You might find yourself wondering what can be done to change
our nation's course. I lay out several options, but I want to be clear
that none of them include violence. Thomas Paine and his fellow
revolutionaries shed their blood so that future generations would
have access to weapons immeasurably stronger than muskets or
bayonets: the weapons of democracy. Those are the tools that we
will use to usher in a second American revolution, a revolution
that won't be fought on battlefields, but in the hearts and minds
of the three hundred million people lucky enough to call America
home.

Important statement —

GLENN BECK'S

COMMON SENSE

THE

CASE

AGAINST AN

OUT-OF-CONTROL

GOVERNMENT,

Inspired by

THOMAS PAINE

GLENN BECK

WITH JOSEPH KERRY

MERCURY RADIO ARTS/THRESHOLD EDITIONS

NEW YORK

Mercury Radio Arts/Threshold Editions
A Division of Simon & Schuster, Inc.
1230 Avenue of the Americas
New York, NY 10020

First Mercury Radio Arts/Threshold Editions
trade paperback edition June 2009

THRESHOLD EDITIONS and colophon
are trademarks of Simon & Schuster, Inc.

Glenn Beck is a trademark of Mercury Radio Arts, Inc.

For information about special discounts for bulk purchases,
please contact Simon & Schuster Special Sales at
1-866-506-1949 or business@simonandschuster.com.

The Simon & Schuster Speakers Bureau can bring authors
to your live event. For more information or to book an event
contact the Simon & Schuster Speakers Bureau at 1-866-248-3049
or visit our website at www.simonspeakers.com.

Designed by Ruth Lee-Mui

Manufactured in the United States of America

5 7 9 10 8 6 4

ISBN 978-1-4391-6857-8
ISBN 978-1-4391-6950-6 (ebook)

Pro Deo, Pro Familia, Pro Patria

A NOTE FROM
THE AUTHOR

Two hundred and thirty-five years ago, a British citizen with only a basic education set off to make a new life for himself in the British colonies. For two years he worked hard and watched as his fellow colonists grew tired of British oppression. Then he decided to act. Using his contacts in the publishing industry, Thomas Paine anonymously released a pamphlet that made the case for revolution using extraordinarily logical, straightforward, indisputable arguments.

He called it *Common Sense*.

Once Paine put his feelings into words, he realized that he wasn't alone. Only seven months passed between the release of *Common Sense* in January 1776 and the signing of the Declaration of Independence. Seven months—a pinpoint in the history of time, but a moment that put the colonies on an irreversible track toward revolution and, ultimately, freedom.

Seven months that changed the world, forever.

Today we find ourselves back in 1776—but this time our path forward isn't so clear-cut. The abuses being perpetrated by our government are just as obvious now as they were then, but instead of rising up with a collective voice, we sit idly by and watch as our hard-won freedoms slowly dissolve into a puddle of apathy, political correctness, and outright corruption.

We feel helpless and alone as we hear confusing debates over obscure issues play out on the airwaves daily. But that's the lie. The infighting and the purposeful division promoted by our political parties is a simple ploy to keep us from uniting. After all, a citizenry that fights among itself over petty differences is too busy to notice the real cause of its problems.

As you read the details of the immense harm that both parties have done to our country, you might find yourself wondering what can be done to change our course. I lay out several options, but I want to be clear that none of them includes violence. Thomas Paine and his fellow revolutionaries shed their blood so that future generations would have access to weapons immeasurably stronger than muskets or bayonets: the weapons of democracy. Those are the tools that we will use to usher in a second American revolution, a revolution that won't be fought on battlefields, but in the hearts and minds of the three hundred million people lucky enough to call America home.

Over the years, many revolutionaries have used sharp tongues instead of sharp knives—and the results have been extraordinary. Martin Luther King, Jr., for instance, once said to his supporters: "The question is not whether we will be extremists, but what kind of extremists we will be . . . The nation and the world are in dire need of creative extremists."

It was inflammatory language, but he meant that it is much easier to simply die for a cause than it is to find inventive, effective means to fight for it. Violence is the easy way out—but it's also a sure path to discrediting everything you stand for, something that those opposed to him found out the hard way.

"Nonviolence is the answer to the crucial political and moral questions of our time," King said while accepting the Nobel Prize.

He continued, ". . . [man must] overcome oppression and violence without resorting to oppression and violence. Man must evolve for all human conflict a method which rejects revenge, aggression and retaliation. The foundation of such a method is love."

History has proven that King was right—and so our new revolution of thought begins right now . . . with you.

Thomas Paine was an unremarkable man living in a remarkable time. He proved that it doesn't take celebrity, stature, or wealth to make a difference—it only takes someone willing to say the things that need to be said. Well, I am no Thomas Paine—he was an extraordinary writer, a renowned motivator, and a heroic patriot—but the words that follow also need to be said, if for no other reason than to ease my own conscience.

If you believe that it's time to put principles above parties, character above campaign promises, and Common Sense above all—then I ask you to read this book, declare yourself a creative extremist, and then pass these words along to others who may agree with something else that Martin Luther King, Jr., once said:

> The hottest place in Hell is reserved for those who remain neutral in times of great moral conflict.

Do not remain neutral. Do not sit idly by. Do not let others speak for you. Silence has gotten us nowhere so it's once again time for our collective voice to make a simple yet powerful demand . . .

Don't Tread on Me.

CONTENTS

THOMAS PAINE'S
COMMON SENSE (1776)

GLENN BECK'S

COMMON SENSE

INTRODUCTION

I think I know who you are.

After September 11, 2001, you thought our country had changed for the better. But the months that followed proved otherwise. We began to divide ourselves and the partisan bickering that had been absent from blood donor lines and church services started all over again.

You sometimes argue with friends about politics, not because you are a political activist, but because you think the issues are actually important. You have strong beliefs, but you also have an open mind and a warm heart.

You try to do the right thing every day. You work hard, you always try to do your best, and you play by the rules.

You have credit cards, but you can make the payments. You have a home, but with a loan you can afford. Maybe you bought a flat-screen television that wasn't exactly a necessity, but you've never been reckless.

You don't have much in savings and your retirement plans have lost a significant amount of money.

You may go to church, but most weekends, you don't really want to—you'd rather sleep in or play with your kids. Besides, it bothers you that people cut each other off in the parking lot right after the service.

You have children and, like all families, you also have your share of problems—but you're making it. You constantly hope that your kids don't notice you're bluffing as a parent most of the time.

You feel like there's not enough time in the day anymore to just be a family. Everyone is always going in six different directions. You know material things don't matter, but you wonder why it makes you feel like a bad parent if your kids don't have certain shoes, the newest video games, or aren't signed up for five different sports teams.

You didn't have anywhere near the kind of stuff that today's kids have and yet you look back on your childhood with a sense of nostalgia and pride. If your family was poor, you didn't know it.

You turn on the television at the end of a long, tiring day and watch as endless analysts in left/right boxes argue about things done by bankers that, in retrospect, now seem implausible. You're worried about what's happening to our economy, but you're more worried about what it means for your family—and you're not sure what to do.

You try to tune out the bickering by watching an entertainment show—but there are times when you're uncomfortable watching them with your kids. You're not a prude, but you happen to think that a three-year-old shouldn't be watching shows that treat sex lightly and mock mothers and fathers. But what can you do? The other shows are worse.

You've taught your children the difference between right and wrong, yet they come home with language and habits that they didn't learn from you. You're shocked to hear what they're learning in school—but you don't make a fuss because they're the "professionals" and you don't want to be one of "those people" anyway. You don't cherish conflict; you just want everyone to get along.

You don't hate people who are different than you, but you stopped expressing opinions on sensitive issues a long time ago because you don't want to be called a racist, bigot, or homophobe if you stand by your values and principles.

You believe in treating people justly and honestly but there is a difference between right and wrong.

You go to bed exhausted almost every night, knowing you have to get up the next day and do it all over again.

You thought that the politicians you supported and defended cared about the issues you do. Then you began to realize that you were wrong—they only care about themselves and their careers. You feel used and betrayed.

You don't think it's right that while you worked hard, lived prudently, and spent wisely, those who did the opposite are now being bailed out at your expense. You realize now that self-serving politicians and bankers built our financial system on a house of cards that, despite the cheery promises and rosy forecasts, is now collapsing.

Now our government, the instigator of our problems, is telling everyone that they have to start sacrificing. *Don't they understand that I already have been,* you think. You weren't the one spending too much or living on money you didn't have. You made decisions rooted in logic while others made decisions rooted in greed—yet now everyone must pay equally?

Yet, despite all of that, you're still willing to sacrifice more because you want America to succeed. But you demand a plan that's based on common sense and that actually has a chance to work.

You've called your congressman a few times in the past, but they don't listen. Now you just scream at the television. It's about as effective as the phone calls.

The light from the television flickers on the darkened room walls—people at tea parties across the nation fill the screen. You don't know how to feel. You want to do something, but that isn't you. You're not an activist. You don't make signs or chant: "U.S.A.! U.S.A.! U.S.A.!" So, you turn off your light and go to sleep.

Every night it seems you are faced with a choice: Do you unplug or do you speak out? Both of those options make you uncomfortable so you do neither . . . and your frustration continues to grow.

The First Step out of Our Comfort Zone

The fastest way to be branded a danger, a militia member, or just plain crazy is to quote the words of our Founding Fathers. I imagine that this is because words have consequences and the words and ideas that those men shared were revolutionary:

> When in the Course of human events, it becomes necessary for one people to dissolve the political bands which have connected them with another, and to assume among the powers of the earth, the separate and equal station to which the Laws of Nature and of Nature's God entitle them, a decent respect to the opinions of mankind requires that they should declare the causes which impel them to the separation.

It is not time to dissolve the bands that connect us to one another, but it is time to dissolve the "political" bands that *separate* us from one another. Even if we disagree on politics, the phrase "I am an American" is not just a collection of words, it is the embodiment of an idea, one that has power only because "We the People" give it power. But somewhere along the way we've forgotten that, so we feel small and helpless as our country drifts away.

Perhaps what we need is a reminder. A reminder of who we are, who is really in control, and, most important, a reminder of how we got to a place that bears less and less resemblance to the America we remember from our childhoods. Let us start by doing what we've been trained for so long not to: let us declare the causes that unite us.

I

THE RESHAPING
AND REDEFINING
OF AMERICA

We did not vote to change the Republic, we voted to change Washington. We wanted the lies, corruption, and childish "but they started it" games to end. Instead we now see that things have only gotten worse and that the "change" the political elite think we wanted was the transition to a system based on entitlements and handouts. It is insult upon injury and a testament to just how out of touch with the common man our two parties have become.

To some, this may feel like a sudden hostile takeover. It is not. This has been coming for a long time and has been moved down the field by both parties—the only real question was which one would put us into the end zone first.

Most Americans remain convinced that the country is on the wrong track. They know that SOMETHING JUST DOESN'T FEEL RIGHT but they don't know how to describe it or, more importantly, how to stop it. But just because you may not know exactly what your gut is saying, doesn't mean what you're feeling is wrong. It's not. Something hasn't been right for a very long time.

America has been slowly pulled off the course charted for us in Philadelphia more than two centuries ago. Through legitimate "emergencies" involving war, terror, and economic crises, politicians on both sides have gathered illegitimate new powers—playing on our fears and desire for security and economic stability—at the expense of our freedoms. And now, after supposedly massive change, not only are we still on the wrong track, but it feels as though our new conductor has just increased the speed at which our misdirected train is traveling.

Is common sense completely dead in America today? Did intellectual honesty have a moonlight clause? We don't have a shortage of capital or liquidity in this country; we have a shortage of honesty and trust. Where are the Americans who will stop talking about the president or the parties and instead start talking about right and wrong? Where are those who will stand up and say, "Common sense still lives at my house and it's about time it is applied again in Washington!"?

America has let thieves into her home and that nagging in your gut is a final warning that our country is about to be stolen. Our Founding Fathers understood that our rights and liberties are gifts from God. They also understood that WE are an intuitive people. If all of that is true, then it only makes sense that He would alert us to our impending loss.

And now He is—shame on us for ignoring Him for so long.

Through blood and sacrifice we have been given the precious gift of self-rule and freedom. But because this gift was simply handed to us, we esteem it far too lightly. Many an erstwhile patriot has sold his birthright for the perceived security of "free government housing," corporate or personal welfare dependency, or by failing to remember the delicate balance between master and minion.

After the signing of the Constitution, Benjamin Franklin was asked by a woman on the street, "What have you given us, sir?" Franklin responded, "A Republic, if you can keep it."

A critical moment in history has come; our Republic is in jeopardy. Can we keep it?

If the answer to that question, as I fear, is "no," then we have no one to blame but ourselves. For too long we have ignored, enabled, or embraced the flawed character of those we've selected to protect and defend our Constitution. By lowering our standards for them, we've lowered the standards for ourselves. We wanted a life of ease, a life of little consequence and high reward. To get it, we repeatedly empowered thieves, liars, and con men, simply because they promised us ease. Now, because we've trained them that repeated injury has no consequence, they've grown bold and fearless. When we do speak up, they ease our pain with pork, a steady stream of entitlements, and financial candy, and back to sleep we go.

We have so little trust in the character of the people we elected that most of us wouldn't invite them into our homes for dinner, let alone leave our children alone in their care. Yet we leave our country and our children's financial future alone in their care. Why?

Common sense tells us that this is national suicide.

Open your eyes! These people are robbing us blind while turning our children against the principles and values we cherish through indoctrination masked as education.

They have set our house on fire and blocked the exits, all the while convincing us that there is nothing to fear because they are the fire department. When will someone cry out with the truth? They're not our saviors; they're the arsonists. They're not rescuing our country; they're destroying it!

To save ourselves from political and economic slavery, we

must first admit what we already know: America has serious problems that transcend this economic crisis. We must also recognize and admit our critical role in helping create these problems. Finally, we must choose to live by our founding principles and rid ourselves of the poison of those who are proven to have broken the law—no one is above it.

In 1776, *Common Sense* woke up Americans to the fact that an oppressive English government was out of step with the Laws of Nature. Paine asked simple questions and encouraged his fellow citizens to look at America's problems and its future with fresh eyes and a healthy dose of simple logic.

I humbly suggest that our government is once again out of step with the Laws of Nature. The government by, of, and for the people has been turned on its head. It is now a government by the government, of the government, and for the government—the people be damned.

It is clear that the so-called political experts in Washington, the business experts on Wall Street, and the self-anointed experts of education and society have gotten it wrong for a very long time. They rely on their Ivy League educations, family connections, and misplaced egos instead of listening to the cabdrivers, mothers, or plumbers. They pay us lip service while stuffing their pockets with our money—content in their belief that average Americans are too dumb to ever notice.

Thomas Paine wrote, "The cause of America is in great measure the cause of all mankind." Those words are as true today as they were then. America is a unique and special place that is a beacon of freedom for the entire world. Do you still believe that? If not—why not? If so, then do you truly think that freedom from tyranny, "the cause of all mankind," is secure?

HISTORY DEMANDS A CLEAR ANSWER. One response leads us to transnationalism and the end of American sovereignty, while the other leads us to a restoration of our liberty. But time is running out. We must answer the question and face the consequences, or our reckless apathy will answer it for us.

THIS IS NOT A QUESTION TO BE LEFT TO THOSE IN WASHINGTON. Most Americans don't know what they believe, or, worse, they don't have any idea how to decide if Washington's "solutions" are the right ones. We cry out "Don't just stand there—do something!" but then we bemoan the result. Instead, common sense should compel us to ask, "Wait, is there a bigger principle at risk by acting so quickly?" In most cases, the answer is a resounding "yes." Inaction is often the best course of action.

"Just doing something" for political expediency may imperil the causes of liberty, capitalism, inventiveness, and the progressive principle of natural selection. Instead, let's do something, but let's make it *the right thing*.

But that's the catch, isn't it? There's no one on television offering the "right thing" to do whose advice you can accept unconditionally—and that includes me. That is why you've got to empower yourself, find your own voice, and rediscover our common principles and values.

If you're like me, you've screwed up many things in your life, but all of that is a prologue to this moment. Those experiences give us wisdom, humility, and a deep sense of the one emotion that many people try so hard to avoid: failure. But those of us who *have* failed understand that it is a necessary step in achieving success—a step that safety nets and bailouts attempt to take a shortcut around.

What the experts and elitists don't realize is that shortcuts have consequences. The result of preventing failure in a country rooted in freedom is a country that is no longer rooted in logic. Laws of economics or nature no longer seem to apply, because they simply change the rules of the game when they don't like the outcome.

Unfortunately, it is all catching up to us. The laws of common sense do not change according to scale. If it doesn't work in your own checkbook, it won't work in theirs. If it doesn't work at your house, it won't work at the White House.

Let's apply some common sense to the lie that "debt isn't bad." There is truth to the idea that some debt is fine. You can have a reasonable mortgage on a reasonable house. But what most people ignore is that debt works only in the context of an otherwise financially responsible lifestyle.

"We will grow our way out of debt" is the answer they give in response. Well, that might be true if you are healthy, young, and at the beginning of your career. But America is not healthy, our population is aging, and our companies are either being taxed to death or run by Washington politicians—most of whom have never run a business or held a job outside of a law firm.

The sad part is that most of us work hard, play by the rules, and just want a fair shake—but we're tired. We're tired of being angry, tired of being lied to, and, quite frankly, tired of being tired. But we are the current guardians of freedom and, because others have let us down, it is now our duty to face the hard truths and do the right thing—no matter the personal cost. The twenty generations who've fought and died to secure our God-given rights of life, liberty, and the pursuit of happiness expect no more and demand no less.

But are we even capable of maintaining a Republic anymore? Are there enough citizens willing to do the hard work that self-rule requires, or have we become a people who would rather be cared for, fed, clothed, housed, and told what's best for us by a parentlike state? Unfortunately, the evidence suggests the latter.

It was bad enough that our leaders sold out our nation's soul in order to print more money—but then we abandoned our post and started following the same path by switching from the gold standard to the debt standard in our own lives. Americans have changed. Our parents and grandparents relied on debt only to buy a home or a car or put someone through college, but we rely on it to live the lives we *think* we have earned. We've bought the false promise made by enterprising politicians that we all deserve the best right now—no matter the cost. Suddenly, our summer vacations, flat-screen televisions, boats, clothes, and dinners out at fancy restaurants were all "purchased" with debt.

Meanwhile, our politicians, global corporations, and money-changers have redefined the American Dream. Many of us grew up not even knowing that we were considered "poor," but now it seems that no one can stand the thought of not being rich. Politicians and the media told us that America is about having the most stuff, the nicest cars, and the biggest homes. Almost everyone, it seemed, was in it for themselves. Compassion, we were told, was a victim of capitalism.

We should now see that for the lie it is. Compassion and capitalism go hand in hand, but compassion does not go with what these people were really promoting: greed. Of course, not everyone fell for their lies—some banks and mortgage companies refused to play the "home giveaway" game. To them, things like debt, income, and character still mattered and they prudently denied unqualified borrowers. And what was their reward? They were labeled racist, greedy, and out of touch with the new reality.

In short, politicians promised us a new, easier way to success and happiness—and too many of us eagerly embraced and promoted it. How did we not see? How did we forget what our parents and grandparents took for granted? There are no shortcuts in achieving and living the American Dream. It takes hard work, relentless dedication to your core principles and values, and, above all, patience. Nothing comes easy; nothing happens fast.

But that kind of sense is just not so common anymore.

The same politicians who promised us the easy shortcut to the good life are now making another false promise. They're going on television and radio each day repeatedly assuring us that if we throw enough money at the problems they created then we can stop our toxic debt spiral without any more pain. People believe them because they want to think that there is still an easy way out of this and that our misguided beliefs about what our lives *should* be like is still within reach.

That lie is now finally coming undone, exposed by time, marketplace realities, and those Laws of Nature that our leaders have tried so hard to break. Yet politicians still insist that no hard choices need to be made and that hardship and pain—which have always been part of the American experience—are somehow no longer necessary (unless, of course, you are wealthy). When asked to explain *why* hardship and pain should not be borne by all, they simply shout louder: "The wealthiest one percent"; "George W. Bush"; "Pay your fair share."

Incendiary class warfare is not a solution, it's a diversion. But nothing can divert us from the reality that our government has proven to be an unreliable and untrustworthy partner in safeguarding the promise of "life, liberty, and the pursuit of happiness."

If you understand the threat to the Republic, it is your duty to wake up your neighbors by asking them to consider some simple questions:

- Do you trust those in power to always tell you the hard truth—*especially* if it would hurt them at election time?
- How is it possible that every president since Jimmy Carter has promised to lower our dependence on foreign oil, but now we import more oil than ever from countries that do us harm?

- Are we to honestly believe that the country that took the idea of a man walking on the moon and turned it into a reality within eight years, or the country that built a transcontinental railroad in seven years (without power tools or machines) doesn't have the ability to completely build the 670-mile fence along our southern border that was promised to us in 2005?

- Why are the same politicians who insist America is a "melting pot" the first ones to insist that different races, nationalities, and ethnicities retain their distinct languages, identities, and practices?

- Why are those who respectfully question the science behind global warming mocked and condemned?

- Do you believe that your elected representatives view themselves as truly being "public servants" who place your well-being above their own?

- Do you believe that those in Washington see your face when they make decisions or, instead, the faces of those who richly contribute to their campaigns?

- Do you believe that our "public servants" have your best interests at heart and will defend your life, liberty, and property?

You know where you stand on these issues. You believe in the promise and future of America. You must heed the call of generations past and commit yourself to becoming part of America's solution. This will not be an easy or popular journey, but by now we've seen that the allure of the "easy" journey is wrong since it often means having to take an even more treacherous road home.

The next time an "emergency" comes along that Washington feels it "shouldn't waste" there will be many voices on all sides shouting directions. Many of those voices will be wrong—and some will even knowingly be wrong. Do not jump in either direction, just stay calm as others panic. It is in no citizen's best interest to follow politicians who use panic, confusion, and hastily crafted legislation to enact emergency powers that they themselves barely understand. Panic will not lead this ship to a safer port, only farther out to sea, into far deeper and more dangerous waters.

You cannot take away freedom to protect it, you cannot destroy the free market to save it, and you cannot uphold freedom of speech by silencing those with whom you disagree. To take rights away to defend them or to spend your way out of debt defies common sense.

I sincerely believe that no discussion or debate is un-American. I agree with the Founding Fathers that it is only on the battlefield of ideas that the best ones can be recognized and ultimately prevail. Only those afraid of the truth seek to silence debate, intimidate those with whom they disagree, or slander their ideological counterparts. Those who *know they are right* have no reason to stifle debate because they realize that all opposing arguments will ultimately be overcome by fact. Yet those who champion massive taxes and spending to fight climate change, for example, do not seem to understand that. If science is on their side, then why should they care who's against them? "The debate is over" is a line that's used only by those who realize they would never win a debate.

In the end, it is not the debate itself, but those preventing it that are truly un-American. Honest listening and, more important, honest questioning is the foundation of the American experiment. We must listen to each other with renewed ears and speak out with passion, while also recognizing the difference between anger and truth.

Unfortunately, there are many in Washington who understand that honest debates will pull back the curtain on the scam they've been perpetrating. They promise transparency but instead deliver ten-thousand-page legislative bills that must be passed before being read or fully understood. They promise openness, but then move quickly, under cover of darkness, to further their agendas.

In March 2008, President George W. Bush told us that Bear Stearns was too big to fail. If we didn't act to save it before the end of the week, very bad things would happen. So we acted. Since then, the list of banks that are "too big to fail" has grown in excess of five hundred and taxpayer exposure from government bailouts now exceeds $12,000,000,000,000.

Worse, those who are in charge of managing all that exposure have already proven their incompetence.

Perhaps you've forgotten that House members once bounced more than 8,331 checks at their own personal bank, the House Bank—forcing it to close due to their own incompetence and greed. Does it strike anyone else as arrogant that the same politicians who couldn't run their own bank are now vested in more than five hundred banks, including some of the largest ones in the country?

Have you already forgotten how our leaders looked us in the eye and pledged to fix their House Bank problem, only to promptly bounce an additional 4,325 checks?

Have you forgotten how no bounced check or overdraft fees were ever charged, because the House Bank didn't impose those pesky and expensive fees that you and I would have to pay given the exact same circumstances?

Does anyone seriously doubt that if it had been a private bank and not members of Congress who'd written twelve thousand bad checks, there would have been never-ending televised hearings, perp walks, and prison sentences? Would it surprise you to learn that not one of the "public servants" who dishonored their office was ever sent to jail but that the House Sergeant-at-Arms, who took the blame for them, was sentenced to twenty-four months?

Of course not—because we've learned that politicians aren't like you and me. They are like some alien life form who believes they are of higher intelligence, don't have to live by the same rules, and have no personal shame.

The same politicians who couldn't operate their own bank now regularly appear on television to tell you and me that they can solve the economic crisis. More lies from politicians who don't think twice about telling them.

Politicians try to frame the ongoing debate as one about increasing regulation on Wall Street and taming out-of-control bankers—but so much more than your 401(k) is at stake. This isn't a debate about money, it's a life-and-death struggle for personal freedom and national liberty. The economy may be the vessel, but it's sailing us toward a complete reshaping of America. Wake up! The chains of economic slavery have been forged by both parties and many presidents, but they are about to snap shut around the necks of our children and grandchildren.

We cannot let our politicians' actions continue to defy sanity, or our collective *inaction* continue to define insanity any longer. We must try something new: peaceful yet pointed action. Our country's circumstances are too grave and the stakes too high for us to sit silently with the *hope* that somehow those who have fought for so long against our founding ideals will somehow realize the error of their ways. And if you think that things would be different if *your* party was in power, or that things will be different now because *your* side won, think again. Both parties have betrayed our founding principles and we have lost sight of the fact that the only side that matters is the one in step with the principles of the Republic.

I am convinced that the source of our collective silence in the face of growing tyranny is not a failure to appreciate the importance of the fight or the threat we're facing. It's not a result of laziness or lack of patriotism, either. Our silence is due to our failure to see any problem or solution beyond partisan politics.

No longer! The light of common sense belongs to all of us, from every party—let us use it to uncover the challenges, treachery, and truth.

II

MONEY
THE REAL OPIATE OF THE MASSES

There was a time when our political leaders inspired America to greatness and motivated us to face daunting challenges with courage and resolve. Our political leaders led us to successfully revolt against the British. They convinced us to defeat Nazism, fascism, and imperialism by fighting it in the homelands that gave birth to those ideologies. They encouraged us in our fifty-year-long struggle against the spread of communism—and they captivated the world as we watched it collapse under its own weight.

There was a time when our political leaders cited their leadership, temperament, experience, judgment, character, and merit in order to gain the trust and support of a skeptical electorate. Today they purchase votes and campaign cash by boasting about the pork they've secured for their pet projects or the billions they've passed along to their powerful political allies.

With a few notable exceptions, our political leaders have become nothing more than parasites who feed off our sweat and blood. They fail to appreciate America's potential or recognize her superiority and instead they view her as just another country to be sucked dry for their own benefit, without regard for the health of the host.

These parasites have fed undetected for years, but our present economic crisis has laid bare just how badly the members of our political elite have squandered our wealth while failing to prepare us for rough times. In good times it was more difficult to see exactly what they'd done to us, but now the true extent of their looting of the national treasury and pillaging of our paychecks has been exposed.

Unfortunately, our financial security is directly related to our national security—and that's why I believe that what some of these people have done is borderline treasonous. They may not have directly sold state secrets to our enemies, but they've successfully put a target on our backs nonetheless. Our enemies rejoice and celebrate at our economic troubles, all the while plotting how to trigger our ultimate demise.

I have claimed, at various times, that socialism and fascism have been on the rise for two administrations now. Call it whatever you want, but common sense will not allow you to claim that it has resemblance to the system our Founders put together. Under President Bush, politics and global corporations dictated much of our economic and border policy. Nation building and internationalism also played a huge role in our move away from the founding principles. Also, in the latter days of his administration, Bush assaulted the American system by, in his own words, "abandon(ing) free-market principles to save the free-market system."

Enough is enough.

We must stop the spending sickness that plagues Washington, and we must stop it NOW! These addicts have racked up $11,000,000,000,000 in national debt, with your family's share of their spending binge coming in at $116,000. Do not expect sympathy or understanding from our political junkies; they just need another fix. One more high and they'll quit. Really, they promise. But we now know that their promises are empty—$12 trillion in bailout, TARP, corporate welfare, and other money is still not enough.

Politicians have forgotten that the money that sits in the federal treasury represents sacred funds purchased through the labor, blood, and toil of millions of faceless Americans who get up early, go to bed late, and miss countless weekends and nights with their families just to make an honest living.

Our leaders brought us to where we are by never saying no to a good spending project. Through their actions they taught the American people that spending money you did not have was not only reasonable, but patriotic. Our solution to September 11 was zero percent financing and a presidential call to "go shopping."

Common sense tells us that you can't solve a debt crisis with more debt or solve a spending crisis with more spending. It's too bad that common sense itself wasn't for sale—that would be the one new federal purchase I'd support.

Debt: How They Purchased Our Silence and Subservience

Each of us innately knows that debt should be avoided whenever possible. Many of us have lived within our means and played by the rules, hoping for a chance to give our children a better life than we had.

Thomas Jefferson knew that government debt was not only bad economic policy but also morally unacceptable because it effectively makes your children responsible to pay for what you bought. He said, "The principle of spending money to be paid by posterity, under the name of funding, is but swindling futurity on a large scale." If that wasn't clear enough, he also said that politicians should consider themselves "unauthorized to saddle posterity with our debts, and morally bound to pay them ourselves . . ."

By spurning this counsel our politicians damned our dreams. They have effectively branded our children as future slaves to our creditors and they've placed our country in a position of servitude to the rest of the world. If we try to escape those obligations through self-serving economic policies, we will be the ones held responsible.

When we place ourselves in debt we have no one to blame but ourselves—and the same holds true for our country. Yes, it was our elected officials who forced us into economic servitude, but didn't we elect them to office, and then keep electing them term after term, even after the magnitude of their gross incompetence became clear? Yes, it was our politicians who negotiated and approved the pork and the spending, but aren't we the ones who sat idly by while they did it?

Our *interest* payment to service our $11,000,000,000,000 in debt now stands at about $26,000,000,000 ($26 billion). Per month. That's over $300 billion a year that will be sent (likely overseas) to our creditors instead of being used to upgrade our schools, roads, or national defense. Common sense tells us that is unsustainable—a country that cannot educate or secure its population is a country that will not be around much longer.

One of the tricks that our leaders have successfully played on us is the illusion of numbers. If I asked you to send me a check for $4,000 you'd probably think about what you could buy with that money (an amazing vacation, new furniture, braces for your child, etc.) and then you'd wonder why on earth you'd send it to me. But when our government asks us for $26 billion *every month* we don't have the same reaction because it doesn't feel personal.

Well, let's make it personal. With one monthly $26 billion interest payment we could fully fund the annual budgets of the Centers for Disease Control ($6.1 billion, annual budget), Coast Guard ($8.7 billion) and the Department of the Interior ($11.1 billion).

With our annual $300 billion in interest payments we could fully fund the Departments of Commerce ($8.1 billion), Education ($68 billion), Homeland Security ($42.3 billion), Housing and Urban Development ($52.3 billion), Energy ($23.2 billion), Justice ($25 billion), and Labor ($49.6 billion) for an entire year.

By 2019, annual interest payments on the national debt will balloon to a projected $806 billion! Why? Because, as you might know from your own credit cards, interest compounds quickly. Making only the minimum payments will result in the unpaid interest being added to our outstanding debt. It's a cycle that's almost impossible to pull out of and the damage to our country will almost certainly be irreversible. That $806 billion is more than what it cost us last year to fund the entire Department of Defense ($583 billion), Veterans Affairs ($86.6 billion), the Department of Transportation ($68.7 billion), and the State Department ($18.9 billion) . . . *combined.*

Where will all of that money come from? Again, the politicians say "the rich!" or maybe "the greedy corporations!"—but if that's our plan, then we are set up for dramatic failure. The total 2008 profits of Exxon Mobil ($45.2 billion), General Electric ($17.41 billion), Wal-Mart ($12.7 billion), and IBM ($12.3 billion) totaled $87.61 billion. If we taxed those profits at 100 percent we still wouldn't even have one-third of the amount needed to pay the annual interest payment—let alone any of the principal!

So what about the wealthy? Look at it this way: if we took all personal income tax revenue from every American taxpayer for the next decade you would still NOT have enough money to pay off the national debt, even if you *exclude interest.* And, as a side benefit, we'd have zero dollars to fund the actual government over those years.

This is modern-day slavery, but instead of being sold to work in the fields our children will be working hundred-hour weeks at their jobs to pay off the debts we've amassed.

Common sense shouts that if this were happening in your home you'd have to stop spending immediately. So what is Washington doing? The exact opposite. They're spending even more.

President Obama announced that his 2009 budget was projected to produce a $1,700,000,000,000 deficit. If you break that down you find that we're spending $4.657 billion every day for a year, which breaks down further to $53,906.64 per second. In the time it takes you to read this paragraph, our government will have spent more than what most Americans make in more than twenty years of work!

Borrowed money has to be paid back—but it won't be us who will have to do it. Our children will question our sanity for spending money we did not have on "bridges to nowhere," skateboard parks, tattoo removal, and other pork-laden projects that politicians stuffed into "must pass" legislation. They will wonder why we tolerated such reckless behavior from our elected leaders instead of holding them accountable.

How will we respond?

Now How Much Would You Pay? The World's Largest Ponzi Scheme

A successful Ponzi scheme is one where early investors are paid with money from new investors. As long as the scammer can continue to sign up new investors, the cycle never ends.

We're told that Bernie Madoff pulled off the biggest Ponzi scheme in American history by allegedly bilking investors out of $50 billion—but that looks like a petty theft compared to the money stolen via Washington's Ponzi schemes.

Social Security is a great example of a "legal Ponzi scheme." Every time you're paid for work, the government takes a portion of your hard-earned dollars to "invest" in the Social Security Trust Fund, where it sits, collecting interest, until you retire and are eligible to start receiving your Social Security checks.

At least, that's the way most of us *think* that it works. The truth is that your money isn't set aside until you retire. In the meantime it's spent by the government and an IOU is put in the trust fund in its place.

Common sense tells us that there is no difference between what Bernie Madoff did and what our government is doing. They took our money, promised us it was safe, and then spent it for their own benefit. But that's where the similarities end—while Madoff is off to jail, our politicians are off to their next cocktail party.

They believe they are above the law—it's time we show them they're not.

Since we now have a trust fund stuffed with nearly worthless IOUs, there is—surprise, surprise—a massive future liability funding shortfall of somewhere around $13.6 trillion. In other words, politicians have promised to pay $13.6 trillion that they don't have to future retirees.

That's basic fraud, but the reason why it's a Ponzi scheme is that we've now hit a tipping point where millions of baby boomers will begin retiring (and collecting). That means that new payments into the system will be used to pay out benefits to older retirees. In fact, the only way out of this (without doubling or tripling payroll taxes—which would be difficult to do given how high the income tax will already have to be to pay down the debt) is to reverse the pyramid. We need fewer people collecting benefits, and more citizens paying into the system.

Americans sense this lie in their gut—which is one reason why young people were twice as likely to believe in UFOs as to believe they would one day receive a Social Security check. And that poll was taken back in 1994, when the prognosis wasn't as critical as today!

BUT WAIT, THERE'S MORE!
Our $100 Trillion Bipartisan Betrayal

Like most out-of-control government programs, Medicare began with the best of intentions: to assist senior and retired citizens with medical expenses.

There are several different parts of Medicare, but only three of them have the potential to contribute to our economic downfall: Medicare Part A, which pays for hospital admissions and visits; Part B, which covers doctor visits; and Part D, which covers prescription drugs. Unfortunately, like Social Security, Medicare is nothing but a massive Ponzi scheme where the number of those who've been promised benefits greatly exceeds our ability to pay for them.

Medicare Parts A and B have combined unfunded liabilities of $68 *trillion*. Despite knowing that Medicare was already hemorrhaging, politicians passed the Medicare Prescription Drug, Improvement, and Modernization Act in 2003, which authorized Medicare to cover prescription drug costs starting in 2006. In less than three years that Act (Medicare Part D) has run up additional unfunded liabilities of $17.2 trillion.

David Walker, the former comptroller general of the United States (meaning he was formally in charge of keeping our government's "books") called Medicare Part D, "probably the most fiscally irresponsible piece of legislation since the 1960s . . . because we promise way more than we can afford to keep."

I think Mr. Walker is being far too generous. It wasn't a fiscally "irresponsible" piece of legislation; it was a borderline criminally negligent one. There is no difference between our government spending money it doesn't have and someone off the street who runs up their credit cards with no intention of ever repaying them. Both are, at best, morally questionable and, at worst, guilty of theft. In this case, it's theft of our freedom, prosperity, and sovereignty.

For anyone keeping track, our politicians have committed future generations to pay a combined $99.2 trillion just for our unfunded Social Security and Medicare obligations. Add in our national debt and interest payments and you'll easily exceed the capability of most calculators.

What this means to you and your family is that, irrespective of how responsible you have been in your purchases, or how frugally you've lived your life, your share of this $100 trillion will work out to around $330,000. A family of four will be saddled with $1.3 million (again, *excluding* all of the other debt we already talked about). The good news is that the typical high school graduate will earn as much as $1.53 million over his lifespan, meaning that you may want to rethink your current family situation and have more kids. Remember, inverting the population pyramid of the Ponzi scheme is the only way out—although it's an idea that common sense should tell you would only delay the inevitable, since all of those children will also retire someday. Global warming experts would also chastise that idea because growing the human population is "irresponsible."

It's clear that neither the Democrats nor the Republicans (champions of Medicare Part D) really care anymore. They know that when all the bills come due they will either be living a comfortable retirement with the proceeds from a fully vested government pension and access to excellent medical care through their own federal health-care plan, or they'll be dead. That's why they have no incentive to do the right thing, just the politically expedient one. And it's also why we should seriously consider strict term limits on *every* politician. No, make that on every public servant—including bureaucrats, administrators, judges, and appointees. No more lifelong tenure for government employees. Maybe the more short-term we make their careers, the more they'll begin to think about the long term.

Social Security and Medicare have been called the "third rail" of American politics—touch it and your shot at reelection is fried. That's too bad, because the truth is that any serious discussion about these programs will have to address three key things, none of which are appealing to anyone: tax hikes, reductions in benefits, and delayed retirement. Politicians don't win reelection by talking about those things, so they do nothing—and they rationalize it by saying that if they lose an election they won't be able to keep fighting for you and your children. I think common sense tells us what to make of that kind of logic.

If politicians really cared they would stop the bleeding. They would stop the spending. But they don't. Whether their patient lives or dies is of no consequence to them, so long as they're reelected.

The lecherous politicians who lied to us about funding Social Security and Medicare are the same ones who are now trumpeting "free" universal health care. And instead of pointing at their track record and laughing hysterically, we sit by and listen receptively, as though this time might somehow be different.

When politicians want money, they traditionally write a bill that provides lots of overly optimistic details about the particular program they want to fund. That's why it's so interesting that President Obama's request for $634 billion to be put into a "universal health-care reserve fund" really doesn't come with a plan about where the money will come from, who will be eligible for it, or how it will be spent.

Common sense should tell us that, given our experience with the Social Security Trust Fund, the very notion of another "reserve fund" is absolute insanity. What business owner could tell his employees that he is going to start a health-care plan, require employees to pay into it, and collect their monthly premiums, all without ever telling them where the money was going or what benefits or exclusions would apply to the plan? That employer would be in jail.

How many of us would make a down payment on a car that we didn't test drive or a home we didn't know anything about? But that's exactly what the lunatics running Washington are now proposing while simultaneously lying to us about the solvency of our Social Security and Medicare programs. Fool me once, shame on you. Fool me twice, shame on me. Fool me for seventy years and bill me $100 trillion while I sit by and accept more of the same? Then shame on all of us for being ignorant and powerless Americans.

If we fail to speak up and speak out against this madness then we should be prepared to accept everything we get. Samuel Adams said that those who prefer the "tranquility of servitude" had best be prepared to "crouch down and lick the hands which feed you." That advice is as relevant today as it was back then. And so are his closing words: "May your chains sit lightly upon you, and may posterity forget that you were our countrymen!"

BUT THAT'S NOT ALL! Act Now and We'll Also Include a Financial Meltdown!

Now that everything is beginning to crash down upon us, what do our politicians do? They promise us that the way out of our crisis is to spend trillions of more dollars in borrowed funds. And we believe their lies because it feels good. We look to any good news to convince ourselves that our ship missed the iceberg and is not really sinking.

But it is sinking . . . and so are the lifeboats.

The boat analogy is apt, not only because we are a stricken vessel that is sinking deep in uncharted waters, but also because we've handed over control of our ship to a captain who works for a hostile, competing shipping company.

The shortsighted political elite brag that China holds $724 billion in U.S. Treasury securities, making it the largest foreign holder of our debt in the world. They talk with pride about how China's willingness to buy our treasury securities reflects their confidence in our economy and future. But what they fail to mention in their carefully orchestrated press conferences is that China is in a position to dictate our future because it can create a crisis here unlike any we've ever seen before. It wouldn't take one missile or army battalion to do it—it would just take a decision by them to sell all of our debt or to demand extravagant interest rates from us in exchange for continuing to buy it—something that many are concerned is right around the corner.

The Ivy Leaguers tell us that will never happen. If China sells our debt it would collapse our economy, thereby eliminating the largest market for their products, meaning a crippling of their economy as well. It's a very logical case—but by now we should know that logic is in even shorter supply among our leaders than intelligence.

Here's how this scenario might play out if it were happening in your own home instead of in Beijing and Washington: You lost your job months ago and haven't told your wife about it. To keep up the illusion of your old life, you've run up all of your credit cards and you're having a hard time even making the minimum payments.

You know your wife will catch on if you stop going out to dinner or shopping so you continue to eat out and buy nice stuff. Months pass and you're now run up more debt than you could ever pay off—even if you get a better job. To make matters worse, you cheated on your taxes and were less than honest when filing your unemployment paperwork.

Now things are starting to come apart at the seams. When bill collectors and IRS auditors call, you blame them loudly in front of your wife, accusing them of incompetence in their record keeping.

As things continue to get worse, you start to believe your own lies. *I'm sure I'll win the lottery*, you think to yourself as you hand over another hundred dollars to the convenience-store clerk. *That would solve everything!*

Knowing that you need to buy time and wait for the next lotto drawing, you borrow money from the only source that will lend it to you: the mob. They tell you that you will have to pay them a much higher interest rate than usual and that you'll have to pay it all back by the end of the week. *No problem*, you think—you'll find a way; you just need some breathing room.

You take the money, confident in your delusional belief that the massive lottery jackpot is yours after the next drawing. While you're waiting, you take your wife out to the casino and lose all of the mob's money. The next day, the lottery numbers are drawn and . . . you lost. Now you owe your creditors thousands, you face jail time for cheating, and, worse, Vinnie will be knocking on your door at the end of the week to collect. One way or another, Vinnie always gets paid.

That is where America now finds herself.

Our solution has been to ward off Vinnie and the others by essentially breaking more laws. We're cranking up our printing presses at breakneck speed—something that is akin to counterfeiting given the fact that we have absolutely no collateral to support any of that money.

Our strategy isn't all that far off from the one used by doctors who fight cancer. They literally inject poison into cancerous cells with the hope that the poison kills the cancer before the cancer kills the patient. It's a delicate balance with potentially fatal results. But doctors take precautions; they have a game plan and an exit strategy. We don't. We're treating our cancer with massive doses of chemo . . . and it's killing us. There is no balance, no plan, no exit strategy, and yet, despite a track record of terrible, life-threatening decisions, we continue seeing the same doctor. When do we realize it's time to find a completely new kind of treatment?

The worst part is that the snakes responsible for this scheme know that it isn't going to work. Why? Because it never has. But they also know that, unlike private corporations or businesses, countries do not go bankrupt, because governments can always print more money to satisfy their debts.

Ask the Germans who lived in the final days of the Weimar Republic or the Africans presently trying to survive day to day in Zimbabwe if hyperinflation is real. Just as in America today, those countries both believed that hyperinflation couldn't happen to them, or that they could contain its awful consequences. They were wrong.

So-called experts cite the historical consequences of grotesque overspending but then go on to conclude that our own destiny will be different from those who previously went down this same path. I'm sorry, did I miss something here? Isn't the definition of *insanity* doing the same thing over and over but expecting a different result? Spending too much money and purchasing our own debt devalues our dollar, the inevitable consequence of which is that it will take more of them to buy what we want. That's called inflation and it is one Law of Nature that the powers-that-be will soon not be able to ignore.

Our legacy to our children need not be a lifetime of servitude to our country's creditors—but the insanity must end now. The time available to save our country will run out well before the money does.

III

THE POLITICAL WEAPON OF CHOICE
THE U.S. TAX CODE

The tax code that started in 1913 as fourteen pages now exceeds sixty-seven thousand.

An income tax that was promised to only apply to the wealthiest 1 percent in 1913 quickly grew to 5 percent in 1939 and then, following World War II, to almost 75 percent of all Americans. To soften the tax blow, the government did what it always does: it reframed the argument. When "War on Terror" was considered to be too aggressive it was changed to "overseas contingency operations," which is supposed to sound much friendlier. The same idea applied to our tax agency. The "Bureau of Internal Revenue" was renamed the "Internal Revenue Service" to, as the government put it, "stress the service aspect of its work."

Talk about smiley-faced fascism.

Six of President Obama's nominees were either tangled up in the tax code's complexity or were simply crooks who sought to defraud the government. But since they were all well-traveled in political circles, Congress graciously excused their tax "issues" as honest mistakes.

But what if they weren't? What if some of the people now working in the highest levels of our government are no different than imprisoned tax cheats Wesley Snipes or Richard Hatch, who conveniently "forgot" to declare the million dollars he won on *Survivor* as income?

Here's the problem: we'll never know because both the media and the people failed the Republic. Why did no one demand that each of these nominees explain their behavior under oath in televised hearings? Why did no one demand that the harshest of penalties be imposed on every one of these people for what they'd done—even if it was a mistake? After all, if you leave some income off your taxes, I'm pretty sure the IRS will not be accepting "sorry," "I forgot," or "I used TurboTax" as an excuse.

And that brings us to admitted tax violator Timothy Geithner. As Treasury secretary, he is the person responsible for not only leading America out of her economic crisis, but also for overseeing the IRS and enforcing the very laws he failed to obey.

Here is a man we were told was the *only person smart enough* for the Treasury job, and yet he wasn't smart enough to pay his payroll tax? He's a "brilliant" economist and yet he wasn't brilliant enough to figure out his tax bill, even though his employer (the IMF) had done the math, cut him a check for the right amount, and made him sign an affidavit acknowledging that the check was to be used for his payroll tax?

Wow. I sure hope he understands a credit default swap a little better than explicit instructions like "Send this check to the IRS."

Congressman Charlie Rangel from New York chairs the House Ways and Means Committee, which means he's responsible for writing the tax code. But, apparently, he's not smart enough to follow it. He allegedly failed to pay taxes on seventy-five thousand dollars in rental income from his villa retreat at the Punta

Cana Yacht Club in the Dominican Republic. His excuse? He didn't know the tax applied to rental properties in the Dominican Republic.

An investigation began under the "most ethical" congressional promise keeper, Nancy Pelosi, who said that a full accounting would be done no later than January 2009. Perhaps they're using the same math to figure their calendars as they used on their taxes, because January came and went, as did February, March, and April—and we still haven't seen a report. But they did find plenty of time to reappoint Congressman Rangel as chairman so that he can continue to oversee the writing of the tax law in the meantime.

If we give all of the people who filed incorrect tax returns the benefit of the doubt and assume that every single one of them simply made an honest mistake, then doesn't common sense tell us that maybe the tax code is just a little too complex?

Our tax code is not just about collecting revenue for the government. If it were, then we would have followed Russia's example (yes, *that* Russia, as in the former Soviet Union) and instituted an easy-to-follow, hard-to-dodge flat tax.

The Russians were having difficulty collecting taxes under a progressive income tax system complete with different tax brackets, deductions, and exemptions. So Russia converted to a flat tax and the results were amazing and immediate. In less than a year the income raised under the flat tax was about 25 percent higher (adjusted for inflation) and voluntary compliance with the law went up.

Unfortunately, unlike the Russians, we work hard each year to make our tax code *even more* convoluted. How bad is it? It now takes Americans about 7.6 billion hours to prepare their taxes. That would be like hiring 3.8 million full-time people just to prepare our taxes and address all of the tax-related issues that we deal with every year. In 2006, Americans spent $193 billion just to comply with the tax code.

Why does it take so long and cost so much? Because the code is changed almost every year—more than five hundred times last year alone. And it's done for two simple reasons:

1. Favors can be done for special interest groups and hidden in the complex framework.
2. The tax code can crush an enemy without leaving any bruises or broken bones and reward allies without leaving a money trail.

Here are the realities of Washington. If you're a friend to those in power and fail to pay your taxes, it's considered a simple oversight and you move on to become secretary of the treasury. But if you're considered hostile to those in power then the same mistake will be used to destroy your reputation. For a recent example, look no further than Joe the Plumber. But this isn't a new political tactic. Do you think it's purely a coincidence that Martin Luther King, Jr., was targeted as a tax cheat or that both Jesse Owens and Joe Louis were investigated for tax-code violations after they spoke out against the government?

A complex and confusing tax code is a weapon that can be used to intimidate enemies (windfall profits tax on oil companies) and punish the innocent but politically unpopular person (a 90 percent tax on corporate executives) while rewarding friends with exemptions, deductions, and individualized loopholes.

It's been said that "the power to tax is the power to destroy," and both the Democrats and the Republicans have used that power irresponsibly for political gain. Too many people in Washington have forgotten how much sweat and blood go into earning an honest dollar. I am convinced that if we could get politicians to spend six months picking fruit, pouring cement, or waiting tables, they'd have a much deeper appreciation of their sacred duty to spend our tax money wisely.

Common sense tells us that if we were required to pay our taxes in terms of physical labor instead of money, we would have put an end to wild spending a long time ago. For example, if a roofer were required to work on twenty new homes instead of paying taxes or if a car mechanic were forced to repair fifty new engines as his debt to the government, we would have rebelled against wasteful spending decades ago. In many ways it's easier to part with our money than our time but common sense tells us that they are one and the same: Time is money.

It's time we take away the ability of Congress to bribe or punish companies by using the tax code. If a company breaks the law, use the criminal code, not the tax code, to punish them. Companies and individuals should rise and fall on their own merits, not on the basis of tax breaks, subsidies, and other goodies that Congress uses to buy votes and bribe voters. And if all else fails, then maybe we should do as Professor Thomas Sowell once suggested and move Election Day to April 16. (Have you ever noticed that Election Day and Tax Day are almost as far apart on the calendar as you can get?) What better way to hold these people accountable for how they spend our money than to decide the fate of their careers the day after we cut our checks?

It's Not the Money, It's the Rule of Law

The Progressive movement (which created the modern income tax under President Wilson) saw America as a democracy rather than what it really is: a Republic. The distinction is not subtle and our Founders were clear in the belief that a democracy always led to mob rule. But the Progressives (both Republican and Democrat) felt that democracy and socialism are twins since both ultimately had their power stem from the people. If the people felt that someone or some group made too much, they could level the playing field for the good of all.

Not much has changed in the hundred years since.

The tax code has never really been about raising revenue as much as it is about punishing opponents, helping friends, or as President Obama says, instituting a system of "fairness." Government bailouts are similar. Did all of those companies *really* need that money, or was it in the government's interest to force it down their throats so they'd have some control over them?

It's what President Obama's chief of staff, Rahm Emanuel, meant when he said, "You never want a serious crisis to go to waste. And what I mean by that is it's an opportunity to do things that you could not do before."

Although Emanuel is a Democrat, that is not a partisan sentiment; Republicans are equally opportunistic.

The rule of law was meant to prevent a crisis from being taken advantage of by forcing outcomes of disputes to be decided according to a strict set of principles, not subject to raw emotion, popularity, political power, or financial clout. But that concept now seems to be just another "traditional value" that people like New York senator Chuck Schumer believes is "over." Consider the following:

- The U.S. House of Representatives used its power to target a group of AIG insurance executives who collected a bonus they were contractually and legally allowed to receive, by passing a bill that would have imposed a 90 percent retroactive tax on their bonus money;
- New York state attorney general Andrew Cuomo threatened to reveal the names of AIG employees who

were paid a contractual bonus and wouldn't voluntarily return that money;

- GM was required to fire its CEO as a prerequisite to receiving any additional federal bailout money even though the CEO didn't engage in any criminal or corporate malfeasance;

- Banking executives were threatened to accept government bailout funds or risk increased scrutiny and audits;

- Government officials are seeking authority to seize any company that could pose—in their sole opinion—a "systemic" economic risk;

- The sacrosanct "secret ballot" is under assault by union leaders who feel it's more important to get new members than protect free elections;

- The government has suggested it will force states to accept federal stimulus money even if they don't want it;

- The state of Connecticut has considered legislation that would *retroactively* raise the state income tax on high-wage earners;

- The rich are being vilified and targeted because they are rich. (Class warfare is always politically popular, but common sense tells us that people won't work if they can't keep what they earn. It also tells us that what starts as government taking on the "rich" always trickles down—remember, in 1913 the income tax was applied to only the wealthiest 1 percent.);

- Executives at AIG, Fannie Mae, and Freddie Mac are all on the federal dole and have received billions in corporate welfare. Executives at all companies received bonuses, but while AIG executives were targeted by Congress and unions, executives at Fannie and Freddie received scant attention due to their ties to government.

Is any of this in accordance with the rule of law? These abuses must stop.

African-Americans have long understood dual justice. One set of laws for whites and one for blacks. While we have made great strides in correcting that injustice, we have gone in the opposite direction with the rest of society. We have allowed the system to be so corrupted that many want justice to be "empathetic," not blind.

When this weed takes hold, it will choke the very life and security out of our system as vengeance and vigilantism become the only available source of "justice." Millions of people who have played by the rules are forced to assist those who haven't and it causes them to question the fairness of a system that lets people reap rewards for risky behavior and prevents them from facing any consequences or losses.

While our current president and political leaders repeatedly assure us that giving government more power is the only answer, George Washington calls out from the past to remind us that government itself is usually the problem: "Government is not reason, it is not eloquence, it is force; like fire, a troublesome servant and a fearful master. Never for a moment should it be left to irresponsible action."

But an increasing number of Americans don't see it that way. A recent poll revealed that a slim 53 percent of Americans believe that "capitalism" is a better system than "socialism." A full one-fifth of Americans think that socialism is the better system and an embarrassing 27 percent are "not sure."

Wake up, America! You have bought into the lie that capitalism is only about money, corporations, greedy businessmen, and corrupt politicians who cut backroom deals. Capitalism isn't about money, it's about freedom—the freedom to try and fail that made the United States the richest industrial nation in the world by 1905 and the freedom that has kept us there ever since.

That is the power of the system that we now seem so eager to trash.

The scariest part of the poll was what it revealed about Americans under thirty—the next generation. Among this group, the results were basically split: 37 percent preferred capitalism, 33 percent favored socialism, and 30 percent were undecided.

There is a lot of work to be done to return America to her founding roots—roots that most people don't even fully understand. The first government established by our Founding Fathers was under the Articles of Confederation, a document that created the weakest possible form of national government. Why? Because they recognized that having no government meant anarchy, but they also knew that government was a "living creature" that would seek to grow in power at the expense of personal freedom. Their compromise was to give America the leanest form possible and let it grow from there.

But it didn't work; the government was too weak. So the patriots made another go at it. Fifty-five men met during the hot and humid Philadelphia summer to hammer out a new document that would give government slightly more control: the Constitution of the United States of America.

When Americans say that socialism is a better system than capitalism they are essentially saying they prefer to be led and fed by the state than be free. They are saying, perhaps ignorantly, that they prefer increased state control over their personal decisions because having a cap on success is an appropriate price to pay for also having a cap on failure.

Those who desire to have their hand held by government admit that they are sheep willing to be shorn and molded by their master—yet their ranks are likely to swell as the economic crisis worsens, because hunger and fear almost always trigger a stampede to security. In this context, the word *security* is defined as "total government"—the type of which is inconsequential, since they've all been proven to be miserable, selfish, and violent masters. A simple reading of the stories told by those who survived under the regimes of Hitler, Mussolini, Stalin, Lenin, Castro, Chávez, or Kim Jong-il should tell you everything you need to know.

IV

THE PERKS AND PRIVILEGES OF THE POLITICAL CLASS

W ould you apply for this job?

Be your own boss. Performance reviews conducted but then immediately shredded! Make mistakes and assign the blame to other people with no consequences. Hefty six-figure salaried position with annual increases automatically granted without regard to work performance. Medical benefits are top of the line and are publicly subsidized. Pension plan is extremely generous and has a very short vesting period. Work onsite 118–184 days a year and then work from home . . . or not! Travel the world and attend elaborate cocktail parties, all for free. Regularly meet people who think you're personally revolting and professionally inept but are forced to call you "sir" or "madam" out of sheer fear.

If the job of a congressman were described candidly and truthfully, only two types of people would apply: Jimmy Stewart's idealist Mr. Smith, or a grifter. The idealist would be drawn to the task of reforming the obvious corruption, and the grifter would be drawn to the power and pleasures of the office.

We need to find more Mr. Smiths, and get rid of the grifters.

Congress: America's Aristocracy

It's kind of ironic that those who are first to play the class card against the rich while positioning themselves as one of "the people" are in fact only $26,000 dollars a year away from becoming "villains" themselves.

While the average American earns between $40,000–$50,000 a year, your congressman stuffs $174,000 annually into his pockets—an amount greater than the salary earned by 95 percent of all American *families*. I don't begrudge anyone for making as much money as they can, unless they do it while also: (a) stealing from me or (b) condemning me. Our politicians are doing both.

Being in the top 5 percent of all American families isn't enough for the aristocrats in Congress, so they also provide themselves with perks like subsidized gym memberships, free parking at Reagan National Airport and on Capitol Hill, plus their own cafeterias where members can eat without being bothered by the "unwashed masses" they purport to serve.

All of that creates a bubble around our representatives that makes it hard for them to understand what life is really like across America. Sure, they say they know what it's like to lose a job or have a home foreclosed on—but even if they "get it" do they really *care* or are they doing what they need to do to win their next campaign?

One way that Congress could've demonstrated their willingness to live like the "average Americans" they claim to represent would've been to comply with the laws they created. In an astounding case of "do as I say and not as I do," it wasn't until 1995 that Congress was forced to fully adhere to these federal laws:

- The Fair Labor Standards Act of 1938
- Title VII of the Civil Rights Act of 1964
- The Age Discrimination in Employment Act of 1967
- Occupational Safety and Health Act of 1970
- The Rehabilitation Act of 1973
- The Employee Polygraph Protection Act of 1988
- The Americans with Disabilities Act of 1990
- The Family and Medical Leave Act of 1993
- The Federal Service Labor-Management Relations Statute
- Veterans' employment and reemployment rights at Chapter 43 of Title 38 of the U.S. Code
- The Worker Adjustment and Retraining Notification Act

What happened in 1995 to force Congress to start abiding by the laws they had passed, in many instances, decades earlier? Two major revolutions, both of which took place a year earlier. First, Democrats, who had controlled the House for forty years, were swept out of power, and second, almost one-third of the House Republicans who ran for office were new candidates. They campaigned on a platform of accountability and had enough critical mass to force their own party to make changes.

In hindsight, the promise and potential of that political revolution was short-lived as idealists gave up or lost their seats and opportunists chose power over principles, but those elections still serve as a reminder that real change is possible when enough people support good candidates, regardless of party.

Politicians never change, and neither does their hypocrisy. Congress is now pushing legislation to make unionizing in the workplace easier. Meanwhile, their legislative staffs remain union-free. They seek to destroy the "secret ballot" for you and me while preserving it for themselves in their closed-door caucuses.

Is it possible they don't want to live under these rules because they know they'll impact their ability to do their jobs effectively? Or maybe it's just that they don't want to deal with all of the union rules, regulations, and bureaucracy? Whatever it is, they seem to have no hesitation about imposing that workplace lifestyle on the rest of us.

When it comes to education, many politicians send their children to the best private or charter schools while blocking programs that would allow others to do the same. James Madison would have been appalled at the double standards we've created:

> [Congress] . . . can make no law which will not have its full operation on themselves and their friends, as well as on the great mass of the society. This has always been deemed one of the strongest bonds by which human policy can connect the rulers and the people together. It creates between them that communion of interests and sympathy of sentiments, of which few governments have furnished examples; but without which every government degenerates into tyranny . . . If this spirit shall ever be so far debased as to tolerate a law not obligatory on the legislature, as well as on the people, the people will be prepared to tolerate anything but liberty.

These people could not be more out of step with the Founders if they tried, and poll after poll shows that Americans despise them for it. So why can't we get the fortitude to just vote them all out and start fresh? Do we really buy their lies that no one else could do their job?

Until we are ready to wipe the slate clean and bring in new leaders who are beholden to no one but us and to nothing but the Constitution, we must demand a political "mutual-assured destruction" policy: every law imposed on the people must apply with equal force to those who passed it.

Politicians: More Staying Power than Cockroaches

Politicians, like cockroaches, are not stupid creatures. Both have an uncanny ability to survive, consume all things living or dead, and can apparently live up to one month without their head—though I would argue that politicians can survive much longer than that.

How is it possible that a Congress with an overall approval rating of 13 percent saw 95 percent of its incumbent representatives win reelection along with 88 percent of its incumbent senators? Common sense tells us those two things cannot possibly go together—yet it happened. Why? Because veteran politicians have written the rules to favor themselves and the two mainstream political parties.

In the 2008 general election, the average incumbent House member raised an average of $1,356,311. The challengers raised an average of $336,585. Incumbent senators fared even better, raking in an average of $8,804,631, while their lowly challengers averaged 87 percent less, or $1,155,599.

No matter how great your message is, it's hard to win an election when you can't afford to get it out there—which is why campaign finance laws have helped the parties become so entrenched. But it's not the only reason for their dominance—there's also redistricting, otherwise known as "gerrymandering." Americans want elections that are open and fair, but the gerrymander is designed to make sure that doesn't happen. How? It's simple: by artificially carving out election districts that favor a particular incumbent or political party. That politician and party then have a much better chance of staying in power.

Politicians can actually decide which neighborhoods, races, religions, and income levels they want in their district. They can even decide which side of a street to draw the line down. In short, they get to choose exactly who lives in their district—which begs the question: Are we choosing our representatives, or are they choosing who gets to vote for them?

The dark gray areas on this image show Illinois Democratic representative Luis Gutierrez's 4th Congressional District. Gutierrez has been serving since 1993 and his district is thirty-nine square miles—look at this and tell me if common sense is still alive in Washington.

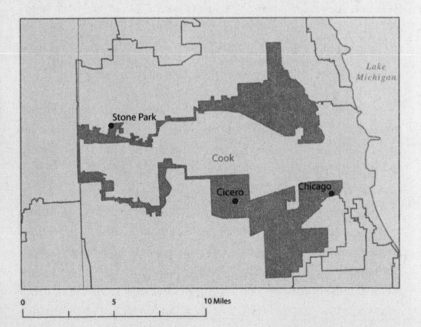

Below is California Democratic representative Grace Napolitano's 38th Congressional District. It covers 105 square miles. Was this district drawn to benefit the citizens who live there, or a particular political party?

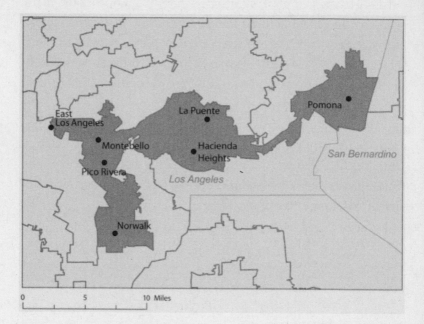

Arizona Republican representative Trent Franks's 2nd Congressional District is shown on the following page. It covers 20,391 square miles, which makes it larger than Rhode Island, New Jersey, and Delaware combined! It's not the distance that's shocking, but how the district's been drawn.

Your voice is diluted when congressional districts are drawn to favor specific politicians or parties. We all want to believe that we can make a difference, that our vote matters—but that's simply not the truth in a growing number of places.

Defenders of these gerrymandered districts would argue that

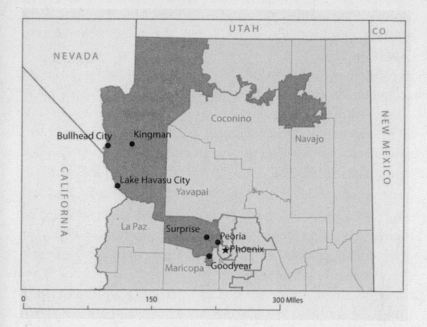

they are lumping people with similar concerns and circumstances together, but isn't that exactly the problem?

Gerrymandering isn't limited to these three districts, and it's used by both parties to create and protect "safe seats." Our Founding Fathers didn't want *any* politician's job to ever be safe or secure; they wanted our representatives to fear the people.

Gerrymandering has another downside as well. By cutting-and-pasting their districts together from large geographic areas, politicians have divided our neighborhoods and destroyed our sense of community. Most likely you are completely oblivious to the boundaries of your congressional district and have no idea if the neighbor across the street from you is represented by the same person. And that's exactly how they want it. By blurring the lines, established politicians can prevent like-minded people from getting together to mount a challenge to them. After all, it's hard to organize a rally when you don't even know what doors to knock on.

Thomas Jefferson understood the importance of bringing communities together in the political process. He proposed creating political divisions called "wards" so that neighbors with similar interests, concerns, and needs could meet and discuss them and then approach their political leaders with a predetermined consensus. As Jefferson put it, "Divide the counties into wards of such size . . . that every citizen can attend, when called on, and act in person. Ascribe to them the government of their wards in all things relating to themselves exclusively." Political divisions that were too large would result in having the "voice" of the people "imperfectly or falsely pronounced."

The simplicity and wisdom of Jefferson's plan is reflected in the layout of many states, which were divided into symmetrical townships of six square miles. Rather than closely mirror that layout, today's politicians have discarded natural boundaries and communal affiliations in favor of Frankensteinian maps that have no foundation in any kind of logic.

Money and gerrymandering remain the key obstacles to "throwing the bums out" and why many members of Congress have served longer than kings and dictators with lifetime appointments. For instance, Senator Robert Byrd has been in that office for more than half a century and Representative John Dingell has been a member of Congress for fifty-three years. Henry VIII of England only served for thirty-eight years. Dictators Stalin and Lenin only eked out twenty-nine and seven years, respectively. Byrd has even served longer than Fidel Castro, who called it quits after forty-nine years!

American politics was designed to push candidates into the political center and away from the outer extremes. Our "winner-take-all" approach was meant to compel candidates to move to the middle in order to pick up the most political support possible. Under normal circumstances, that would also be why our two major parties are so similar to each other—they're both competing for the same block of voters. But these aren't normal circumstances. Instead of competing in the center, our political parties are competing on the fringe. That's not where the voters are, but that's where the *voters who matter* are. Since gerrymandering allows politicians to basically handpick their constituencies, campaigns really only need to be focused on swaying those people.

Our system wasn't designed to operate that way. After George Washington's first two terms, Americans begged him to continue his service, but he refused, believing it would set a bad precedent. Jefferson, citing Washington's example, also refused to serve a third term, noting that "history shows how easily [long-term public service] degenerates into an inheritance."

Of course, FDR didn't care about Washington's or Jefferson's concerns. He stayed on for four terms—a reign that went so well that we followed it up by ratifying the 22nd Amendment, ensuring that it would never happen again. Today our latest political royalty, the Kennedys, Bushes, and Clintons, would never think of getting out of "the family business" for the good of the country (and don't let them kid you—"family business" is exactly what it is).

We are again at a crossroads. The power of the president may be limited, but the power of those entrenched as the "political elite" in Washington is out of control. That is why it is now time to do something that our politicians are quite familiar with: we have to change the rules of the game.

Instituting term limits on *all public servants* is the only way to limit the damage that can be caused by those who lack the character needed to assume such a role. Ben Franklin insisted that service to your country not be a full-time job or career—and he was exactly right. Our public servants must be sent back into private life without the obscene perks they're used to.

Will term limits result in good politicians being thrown out of office too early, the proverbial baby with the bathwater? Absolutely—but that's a small price to pay for the freedom this will grant us. Freedom from corruption, greed, arrogance, and, most of all, freedom from those who put their careers above their country.

Our part in this is simple: You must seek out and support those candidates who strongly support serious term limits. Any candidate who campaigns on the idea that their job is a temporary one is a candidate worth looking closely at. We must also elevate the question of term limits to the same stature as global warming, immigration, taxes, or any of the other issues that will no longer matter if we lose our Republic.

Political Parties: Dividing the People but Taking Us to the Same Place

It wasn't long ago that I believed our political parties actually stood for something. On second thought, I guess I still believe that they stand for *something*, it just isn't the something that I thought.

The only principle that our parties really seem to care about now is a principle called "Get elected at all costs." That's it. Do not believe their lies and propaganda that our parties still matter— they don't. What matters are the values, judgment, and temperament of the candidates—not their party affiliation. You can find values and principles in individuals in any party and you most likely can find criminals, sleazebags, and early-stage sociopaths in any party as well.

More and more people are recognizing that political parties are intentionally causing problems so that they can later attempt (and fail) at fixing them. The greater our problems, the more we're supposed to need them around. But, like so much else, that's a lie. The number of Americans calling themselves "independents" has climbed from 11 percent to 25 percent over the past twenty years, a promising sign in the battle against the two-party system.

If you are still brainwashed by a particular party, it's time for a reassessment. An alternative to the two-party system already exists, given the 25 percent who call themselves independents. It just needs to be taken advantage of. Times are too perilous to substitute blind allegiance to any political party for independent thinking!

That last paragraph also goes for any politician who may be reading this. Democrats who believed President Bush was spending us into an unstable third-world economy, WHERE ARE YOU NOW? Stand up. The people will support you. And Republicans, do you really think that George W. Bush's defense policies were all we cared about? For those who believe our Republic is now at stake, DECLARE YOUR INDEPENDENCE.

We vote for Republicans and get bigger government and more spending. We vote for Democrats and get bigger government and more spending.

We vote for candidates from both political parties who promise ethical government and the Republicans bring us the House intern scandal and the Democrats bring us Charlie Rangel, ethics-plagued Fannie Mae, and Chris Dodd's sweetheart mortgage deals.

We support candidates who tell us they want transparency and accountability, yet we still can't find out who is behind pork projects or who slipped last-minute amendments into legislation.

Are any additional broken promises needed for us to finally realize that these parties all come from the same contaminated source? Both have been infected with progressivism—the belief that your individual rights are subservient to government power and that no personal liberty is above sacrificing for the greater good (a term that is conveniently defined by government politicians and bureaucrats).

Our collective experience since the Founding has taught us that all governments of every stripe are fascist in nature. They will gobble up as much money, resources, and people as possible unless adequately checked. Governments are never static; they always grow. Communism, fascism, socialism, imperialism, and statism are all different ends accomplished through the same means: totalitarian, absolute government control over the individual. All these "isms" simply reflect the mistaken belief that progressively larger governments are needed to address our problems.

The two-party system is a distraction, a sideshow designed to grab and keep our attention by producing a lot of "heated" debate, arguments, and political attacks while accomplishing very little. The best analogy is the movie *Ocean's Eleven*, where a group of thieves rob a Las Vegas casino. The getaway van, controlled remotely by the thieves, pulls out of the casino parking lot and is followed by the police to a deserted parking lot. But it's just a red herring. The thieves aren't in the van, they're still in the casino, free to walk out the front doors with loads of cash while the police are distracted.

Our politicians are destroying the economy. They are hijacking private business and are stealing our money and our children's future. Bush did it. Obama is doing it now. But we're fooled because we're distracted by red herrings, such as debates over which party is *more* irresponsible.

I expect Democrats to attack this book's message and messenger because they will believe that it's pointing fingers at them. I expect Republicans to attack the message and messenger as well for similar reasons. Both would be 100 percent accurate.

Make no mistake, this is a fight of Us versus Them. "Us"

comprises those who believe in liberty, as described in the opening lines of the Declaration of Independence. "Them" comprises those who believe that the definition of *liberty* must evolve with the times.

Politicians, I have a message for you: Americans do not care about the *R* or *D* after your name; in fact, those letters probably hurt you. We care about your character. Americans don't want someone with whom they always agree, but someone they can always trust. We want to be a part of a process that is open, transparent, and fair—but, most of all, we just want you to do what you promised you would. We'll call you with our thoughts when we can, but if you keep your end of the bargain, then you'll have nothing to worry about. We'll always be there to watch your back.

Let us be the radical thinkers of our day and remember the commonsense warnings that George Washington gave us in his farewell speech:

> The common and continual mischiefs of the spirit of party are sufficient to make it the interest and duty of a wise people to discourage and restrain it. It serves always to distract the public councils and enfeeble the public administration. It agitates the community with ill-founded jealousies and false alarms; kindles the animosity of one part against another; foments occasionally riot and insurrection . . . A fire not to be quenched, it demands a uniform vigilance to prevent its bursting into a flame, lest, instead of warming, it should consume.

We are now experiencing exactly what George Washington warned us about. Neither party is serious about finding solutions. Their focus is instead on building their own tiny political empires where "their guy wins" while the country burns. That is not leadership, THAT IS NATIONAL HOMICIDE. They seek to incite political support or raise money by pitting us against each other on issues like abortion, gun control, immigration, and gay marriage because they know that by igniting heated arguments, the issues are less likely to be solved and their careers are more likely to be secure. Every time you vote "against" someone rather than "for" someone the two-party system wins and America loses.

When we support or vote for candidates outside the two major political parties we are immediately lectured about wasting our vote or making it easier for the less desirable of the two major candidates to claim victory. These lies are repeated every election and they must be ignored.

You never waste your vote if you vote your conscience. Need proof? Just look at Arlen Specter. In the 2004 election, two third-party candidates ran, both of whom were considered far more conservative than Specter. But most conservatives figured those minor party candidates would never win, so they sold out their own values and voted for someone who very few people considered to be a true conservative.

Nearly five years later, Specter switched from the Republicans to the Democrats. So I ask you: who wasted their vote, the four percent of people who went with the candidates from the Constitution and Libertarian parties, or the 53 percent who voted for a man who later stabbed them in the back by switching parties simply to have the best shot at winning his next election?

Common sense tells us that supporting the individual of our choice, after having studied his position on the issues, is never a waste. Are truth, honesty, and candor any less desirable in candidates that don't happen to be Republicans or Democrats? Stop believing their lies!

The enemies are at the gate, and have been for quite some time. Many "liberals" have begun to call themselves "progressives" instead because it sounds new and forward thinking—but the truth is that it's anything but. It is a movement that requires Americans to sever the ties to our founding and follow an ever evolving social gospel instead.

Common sense tells us that a government that can provide everything is a government capable of taking everything. Wake up! We don't need a new party in power—we need a new way forward!

Enough About Them, How About Us?

The American people are like the suckers in the horror movie who always seem to do the stupid thing while the audience is shouting, *Don't open that door, don't go there!* But for a short time, we actually listened. We didn't open that door and instead we remembered who we really are.

September 11, 2001, changed us as a country. Do you remember the lines filled with Americans who wanted to donate blood—even though none was needed? Do you remember that the following Sunday's football games were postponed, that the late-night comedians deferred their jokes, and that even trial lawyers respected a self-imposed moratorium on terrorist-related lawsuits?

After 9/11 we began to remember our heritage and the power of sacrifice. We returned to our churches, synagogues, and mosques. We reconnected with our neighbors, our friends, our families. Four months after those attacks, 61 percent of us believed our country had changed for the better.

But shortsighted politicians, professors, businessmen, and other "experts" who saw America as a giant shopping mall didn't like the changes. If people were getting to know each other again, they couldn't be buying stuff. And if people stopped buying stuff, then the whole Ponzi scheme would collapse far sooner than those experts had expected.

The same television executives who have filled our sets with acts of violence, murder, and sex took the video of the planes crashing into the towers off the air because they were too "offensive" or "painful" for most people to bear.

It was another lie—but it worked. We stopped thinking about 9/11 and how fragile our freedom is and instead we followed President Bush's advice to spend money and "Get down to Disney World in Florida . . . Take your families and enjoy life, the way we want it to be enjoyed."

The result is that about only 21 percent of us now believe our country is better off today than it was before September 11. We've gone back to being September 10 people—our heads are once again buried in the sand and our hands are out, waiting for the next entitlement paid for with "free government money."

California is a prime example of that. Their budget went from $75 billion to $145 billion in about ten years—a 92 percent increase in state spending. Then their house of cards came crashing down. California was short about $42 billion on their last budget, yet they still won't do the commonsense things to get back on track, like lifting restrictions on offshore oil drilling. In fact, they're doing the opposite—using the same kind of financial schemes that got them into the mess to get out of it. Their latest act of genius is to sell bonds to themselves—something that is akin to borrowing money from your wife. If they won't sacrifice for themselves, why should the rest of the country sacrifice for them?

We are once again living in days that will "try men's souls"; days that will be remembered by historians as great and perilous. But how will history remember us? Will we be remembered as the heroes of our time or as those who lost that which was most precious in order to satiate our own desires and appetites?

V

THE CANCER OF
PROGRESSIVISM

Many people will hear the word *Progressive* and immediately think of liberals or Democrats—but they're not synonymous. Progressivism has less to do with the parties and more to do with individuals who seek to redefine, reshape, and rebuild America into a country where individual liberties and personal property mean nothing if they conflict with the plans and goals of the State.

If the Progressive cancer were limited to defined political systems, it would be fairly straightforward to isolate it, treat it, and eventually be free from the disease. But it's not. It's infiltrated both political parties and the entire political class—the bureaucrats, lobbyists, trade unions, and corporations that all look at government as their own personal ATM machine. The Progressives weren't interested in taking over the political parties, because that kind of thinking was too small; they wanted their movement to engulf the entire country.

The Progressives on the right believed in Statism and American expansion through military strength, while the Progressives on the left believed in Statism and expansion through transnationalist entities such as the League of Nations and then the United Nations.

Progressivism is why, with few exceptions, Americans feel as though the candidates they get to choose from are pretty much the same. Do you elect Progressive candidate A, or *really Progressive* candidate B?

One of the hallmarks of Progressive thought is the concept of redistribution: the idea that your money and property are only yours if the State doesn't determine that there is a higher or better use for it. You can see that kind of thinking in the words of onetime *Republican* president Teddy Roosevelt, who gave a speech titled "The New Nationalism," in which he spoke about "human welfare." Personal property, Roosevelt said, is "subject to the general right of the community to regulate its use to whatever degree the public welfare may require it."

His thoughts on accumulated wealth were equally as surprising. In the same speech, Roosevelt said, "We grudge no man a fortune in civil life if it is honorably obtained and well used. It is not even enough that it should have been gained without doing damage to the community. We should permit it to be gained only so long as the gaining represents benefit to the community. This, I know, implies a policy of a far more active governmental interference with social and economic conditions in this country than we have yet had, but I think we have got to face the fact that such an increase in governmental control is now necessary."

As a perfect reflection of that attitude, you should remember that Teddy Roosevelt not only endorsed a progressive income tax, but was also the first American president to call for national health insurance.

Woodrow Wilson, a Democrat, was the next president to further the Progressive agenda. Like Roosevelt, Wilson didn't believe there were any restrictions on government's power. "For it is very clear," he said, "that in fundamental theory socialism and democracy are almost if not quite one and the same. They both rest at bottom upon the absolute right of the community to determine its own destiny and that of its members. Men as communities are supreme over men as individuals . . . Democracy is bound by no principle of its own nature to say itself nay as to the exercise of any power . . . The difference between democracy and socialism is not an essential difference, but only a practical difference—is a difference of organization and policy, not a difference of primary motive."

These two presidents serve as the idols and philosophical foundations for their respective parties—yet both wanted far more government control. (Roosevelt: "It has become entirely clear that we must have government supervision of the capitalization, not only of public-service corporations, including, particularly, railways, but of all corporations doing an interstate business.") Perhaps that explains why those same parties today seem to continually produce the same results—irrespective of what they promise on the campaign trail.

Like today, the early-twentieth-century Progressives loved to rely on "experts" and used them as an excuse for expanding their power. When Progressives brought America the Federal Reserve System, it was so that our banking and financial industries could be regulated by experts. When they brought us increased government interference in the classroom, it was because education experts knew better than parents how best to teach our kids. When they brought us land conservation, it was because experts had figured out that we were abusing the land. And when the first waves of the Nanny State began to appear, it was because experts had decided that we were drinking too much (Prohibition), not paying enough taxes (introduction of the progressive income tax), and spending our money on the wrong things (redistribution through the tax code).

And it hasn't ended yet.

In 1991, the Progressive Congressional Caucus was formed and its roster of members now includes over seventy representatives and one senator. Their power and influence is reflected in the fact that half of all House standing committees are chaired by members of this caucus. These politicians may be the most outspoken and radical members of the Progressive movement, but they're not alone. There are plenty of others in Congress who share some of the basic ideologies but don't publicly declare themselves Progressives.

For example, consider former president George W. Bush's defense of the massive wealth redistribution that took place through his Medicare Prescription Drug Benefit Plan (Part D). "If you're a low-income senior," he said, "the government's going to pick up a significant portion of your tab . . . If you're an average-income senior, you're going to see your drug bills cut in half." Of course, when Bush said that the government would be picking up the tab, he really meant that the tab would be paid by American taxpayers and their children and grandchildren.

When Hillary Clinton was asked if she was a liberal during the nationally televised presidential debates, she responded that she preferred "the word *progressive*, which has a real American meaning, going back to the progressive era at the beginning of the twentieth century." She went on to say, "I consider myself a modern progressive, someone who believes strongly in individual rights and freedoms, who believes that we are better as a society when we're working together." That should have been a marching order to Americans to go back and read the history of the early-twentieth-century Progressive movement.

Even John McCain, the "conservative" candidate, once said that Theodore Roosevelt was one of his favorite presidents. And you still wonder why it feels like elections offer us no real choice? These candidates may come from different political parties, but their philosophy of the government's role all came from the same corrupt well.

The presidential election of 2008 was truly a repeat of the presidential election of 1912, in which America was really only offered a Progressive Republican and a Progressive Democrat as candidates.

Parallels between the words and actions of our current president and those of our Progressive forefathers aren't hard to find, either. Woodrow Wilson once said, "We must demand that the individual shall be willing to lose the sense of personal achievement and shall be content to realize his activity only in connection to the activity of the many." That sounds eerily like President Obama's campaign answer to Joe the Plumber, who was worried that his taxes would rise. "It's not that I want to punish your success," Obama told him. "I just want to make sure that everybody who is behind you, that they've got a chance to success, too. I think when you spread the wealth around, it's good for everybody."

As I said before, Progressives didn't simply want to create a new party, they wanted to usher in a new form of government. After all, elected representatives were fallible because they were selected by ordinary people instead of those trusted "experts." But those weren't just words, they were a call to action. The Progressive era was an immediate manifestation of that call, but it was far from the end of it. Over the last century, Progressives have successfully moved our country toward more government control and less personal freedom—and they're still pushing the envelope.

I want to be clear: Progressives are not doing this as some sort of master plan to take down America. In fact, it's just the opposite—they love their country and genuinely believe that this is the best way forward. The problem is that there are fewer and fewer people able to stand in their way because we don't teach real American history any more, let alone the real history and vision of the Progressive movement. The principles of freedom and liberty and the beliefs of our Founding Fathers have basically been white-washed from the curriculum, leading to generations of Americans who have no idea what people like Wilson or Teddy Roosevelt really stood for.

The Progressives view the Constitution as a living organism that evolves with time and changes depending on circumstances. Both the Progressives and the Founding Fathers view the Constitution as a set of handcuffs—but the difference is that our Founders believed that it was the power of the State that was to be cuffed, while Progressives believed it was individuals who were cuffed to the greater good of the group. One of those two positions will eventually win out and that will dictate how future generations live their lives.

The battle between these two philosophies is taking place right now in all areas of our lives, but there are a few key issues that Progressives are using to drive their agenda forward: the environment, gun control, education, and religion. As we go through each of them, consider how our leaders have bypassed the idea of massive, overnight change in favor of reshaping our opinions slowly over time—a concept that James Madison warned us about well before Progressivism had even been given a name:

> I believe there are more instances of the abridgement of free-
> dom of the people by gradual and silent encroachments of
> those in power than by violent and sudden usurpation.

GLENN BECK'S *COMMON SENSE* 69

The Right Kind of Green

Despite what Al Gore probably thinks, he didn't create the "green movement." Back in the early 1900s there were several types of electric cars competing with Henry Ford's gasoline-powered Model Ts, and car companies have been seriously experimenting with hydrogen-based fuels since the 1970s.

But while Gore didn't invent the idea of environmental responsibility, he did, along with politicians like George W. Bush, John McCain, and members of the Congressional Progressive Caucus, figure out a way to use it to further his Progressive agenda.

At first glance, climate change and "going green" don't seem like issues that relate to the battle playing out for our country's soul. But that's because we often look at them in a vacuum. If you back away and see the forest instead of the individual trees, you quickly realize what is really going on: leaders who want more government control over our businesses, economy, and personal lives can't simply snap their fingers and get it—they need a vehicle to take them there. My contention is that climate change is that vehicle.

Not surprisingly, the conservation movement came into its own during the Progressive period. The Sierra Club was founded in 1892 and, just twenty years later, Theodore Roosevelt proclaimed, "There can be no greater issue than that of conservation in this country." Today we have Al Gore preaching the same gospel to a different audience. But instead of trying to convince adults who may be set in their ways, he smartly appeals to the feelings and instincts of minors. During an inauguration celebration for President Obama, Gore spoke to a group of thirteen- to seventeen-year-old honor students. He explained to them that current day anti–global warming sentiments are a lot like racist sentiments were decades ago. He told them, *Look, there's a lot of things you understand instinctively but your parents don't understand those things because they're just too trapped in old thinking.*

Do these men truly believe in what they're saying? Do they honestly believe that the environment can really be "saved" through government intervention or is the environment just a vehicle toward the Progressive ideal of total government rule?

Like Gore, Roosevelt didn't just use words, he demanded action. He limited personal freedom and ignored states' rights by giving government more power over water and grazing rights, creating over fifty bird preserves through executive order, and, with the stroke of a pen, establishing more than twenty national forests. It didn't matter to him that businesses, individuals, and states were negatively impacted by each of these decisions or that their rights to those previously public areas were taken away. Roosevelt argued that, as he put it, "the greatest good for the greatest number" required such action. "The New Nationalism," he said, "puts the national need before sectional or personal advantage."

We hear the same arguments today. Politicians lecture us that jobs must be sacrificed and factories closed for the sake of "the greater good." We are told we can't drill for oil, develop nuclear power, or burn clean coal because of the environmental impacts. We are told by our president, "We can't drive our SUVs and eat as much as we want and keep our homes on seventy-two degrees at all times,"—words that eerily echo Teddy Roosevelt's calls for a "new spirit of service, a new spirit of sacrifice . . . where each of us resolves to pitch in and work harder and look after not only ourselves but each other."

In the 1970s, Progressives used "global cooling" as their call for action. That call included, naturally, increased government control. In the 1980s, as science refuted claims of global cooling, Progressives argued for more government power and control to fight "global warming" instead. Today, desperate to explain long periods of cooler temperatures, increased ice formations at the southern polar cap, and other inconvenient "global warming" truths, Progressives now tell us that government must have the power, resources, and money to fight "climate change"—whatever direction that change might be.

We are told that humans are destroying the planet and that only scientists (the "experts") or the very rich, very famous, or very powerful can save it. I guess maybe those people are so busy flying on their private jets attending international climate conferences and accusing us of poisoning the planet that they either don't notice their hypocrisy or they accept it as the price for the great work they're supposedly doing.

We don't trust the political class because they no longer find shame in their own hypocrisy.

As always, the hypocrisy is loudest in Washington. In 2007, Speaker of the House Nancy Pelosi announced with great fanfare that Congress was "going green" by replacing twelve thousand incandescent lightbulbs with environmentally friendly compact fluorescent ones. Trees would also be planted and carbon offsets purchased.

What you didn't see in her press conference was the carbon-belching Capitol Power Plant that burns more than seventeen thousand tons of coal each year. The plant's proud owner? None other than the United States Congress. Since Congress owns the power plant and Speaker Pelosi controls the House, isn't she ultimately responsible for the multiple Clean Air Act violations that the plant's been cited for?

Congress apparently felt it could operate the power plant guilt-free because it purchased close to ninety thousand dollars worth of carbon credits. Those credits allow an entity to emit carbon in exchange for paying another entity to offset that carbon by planting trees or sequestering CO_2, thereby eliminating or reducing the same amount of carbon. This year, Nancy Pelosi's much heralded plans for a carbon-neutral guilt-free Congress died an unceremonious death. Congress will no longer purchase carbon credits. No reason was given for the change, but perhaps Congress was embarrassed by the revelation that several of the companies hired to offset their gluttony had *already* reduced their carbon outputs long before they were contracted by Congress to do so. In other words, if you give someone a thousand dollars to plant ten trees, but later find out that they planted those trees five years ago, have you really done anything to help the environment or are you just helping your own conscience? In Congress's case, it was definitely the latter.

Common sense tells us that the simpletons running our government should have learned from their own failed two-year experiment with carbon credits that the system does not work. But instead they've come to a different conclusion. They've decided that while they will no longer purchase carbon credits, American businesses and corporations must start to.

In the same month that they abandoned carbon credits, Congress introduced a 648-page bill that could effectively impose the carbon-credit scheme on every American business. Yet, in all of those pages, two simple questions are not answered: Who will be taxed, and how will the money that is raised, in what one politician called "the most significant revenue-generating proposal of our time," be spent?

What *was* included in the bill were explicit details of new efficiency standards—such as protocols for putting on a "slanted roof" that could require "fiberglass asphalt-shingle roofing." There were also ten pages discussing "portable lighting," including a section on "art work light fixtures," and another section spelling out the details of standby power needed for hot tubs.

The hubris, arrogance, and hypocrisy of politicians has no limits. They seek to impose laws on us that they themselves cannot tolerate. It's a return to the "do as I say, not as I do" mentality, and it's taking us down a subtle road to tyranny.

The Lightbulb Lie

WARNING: This product contains a chemical known to the State of California to cause cancer.

WARNING: This product contains a chemical known to the State of California to cause birth defects or other reproductive harm.

Sounds like a nasty, dangerous product, right? It is. The product is mercury and it can be toxic, which is why California wanted those two warnings posted on cans of tuna.

But if mercury is so dangerous, then why would Congress require that mercury-filled lightbulbs be used in our homes, offices, hospitals, and churches starting in 2012?

Compact fluorescent light bulbs (CFLs) contain an average of four milligrams of mercury each, far more than the .12 milligrams contained in a can of light tuna.

It gets worse. The lightbulbs these self-serving politicians decreed must be used in your home in order to save the environment are so poisonous that the Environmental Protection Agency actually created cleanup procedures to be followed whenever a CFL is broken. Here are a few highlights:

- Before Cleanup: Air Out the Room
  - Have people and pets leave the room, and don't let anyone walk through the breakage area on their way out.

- Open a window and leave the room for fifteen minutes or more.
- Shut off the central forced-air heating/air conditioning system, if you have one.

- Cleanup Steps for Carpeting or Rug
  - Carefully pick up glass fragments and place them in a glass jar with metal lid (such as a canning jar) or in a sealed plastic bag.
  - Use sticky tape, such as duct tape, to pick up any remaining small glass fragments and powder.
  - If vacuuming is needed after all visible materials are removed, vacuum the area where the bulb was broken.
  - Remove the vacuum bag (or empty and wipe the canister), and put the bag or vacuum debris in a sealed plastic bag.

- Cleanup Steps for Clothing, Bedding, and Other Soft Materials
  - If clothing or bedding materials come in direct contact with broken glass or mercury-containing powder from inside the bulb that may stick to the fabric, the clothing or bedding should be thrown away. Do not wash such clothing or bedding because mercury fragments in the clothing may contaminate the machine and/or pollute sewage.

- Disposal of Cleanup Materials
  - Immediately place all cleanup materials outdoors in a trash container or protected area for the next normal trash pickup.
  - Check with your local or state government about disposal requirements in your specific area. Some states do not allow such trash disposal. Instead, they require

that broken and unbroken mercury-containing bulbs
be taken to a local recycling center.

One woman who had the misfortune of breaking a compact fluorescent light bulb in her home was told by her state department of environmental protection that the spilled mercury levels were six times higher than the state's "safe level" and therefore a cleanup performed by a professional hazardous material team should be considered, at a cost of several thousand dollars.

At least we now know how many agencies it will take to change a CFL: two—the local department of environmental protection and the local hazardous-material disposal unit.

If you bury your head in the sand and believe that things will just get better on their own, that you will one day wake up and government will have decided to simply leave you alone—then you deserve to see your children wearing the chains of government servitude.

Each and every "feel-good" environmental policy has a price attached to it. Politicians and extremist environmentalists never talk about the cost of carbon credits, or CFLs, or "cap and trade" programs, but not talking about it doesn't make the cost any less real. For example, in his latest book, Professor Thomas Sowell talks about how homes were far more expensive in cities and towns that adopted environmental "smart-growth" and "open space" policies. Why? Supply and demand. By imposing an "artificial restriction" on developable land, the cost of buildable land rose. It's another example of the difference between feeling and thinking—open space *feels* good, but once you *think* about it you realize there's a substantial hidden cost.

Climate change has all the components needed to be an issue used to reshape America: massive support from the younger generation; a feel-good quality to it that people feel guilty for opposing; ties to the most important, most influential global corporations and leaders; ties to the world's energy supply; and, most importantly, trillions of dollars at stake.

How many people did Michael Moore speak for when he said that Obama "has the massive will of the American people behind him" and had been granted "permission by us to do what he sees fit"? That is simply not the way our republic works—a person who does "what he sees fit" is not a president, he's a dictator. We cannot allow the Michael Moores of the world to speak for us.

Isn't it amazing that the law does not require one human being to save another human being from injury or death? If you see a stranger, or even a relative, drowning in a pool, the law doesn't impose any obligation on you to save them, even if you could do so without any risk to yourself. Yet the same legal system requires you, under threat of penalty, to recycle, to avoid letting your car idle, and to put CFL bulbs with poisonous mercury into your homes—all to save the environment. Common sense tells us that any legal system based on such grotesquely misplaced priorities is one that cannot endure for long.

The endless laws, rules, and regulations (fifty-one thousand new ones have been added since 1995) already on the books, along with the ones that are still coming (like "cap and trade") are not really about breaking your bad habits—they're about breaking your spirit. They're about sending you the message that you are no more important or significant than the spotted owl or a salt-marsh harvest mouse.

These laws are a stark reminder that your significance as an individual, even as a human being, depends on the recognition you are granted by the state. We are all being trained that we are simply a small part of a much larger community made up of "humankind," along with trees, plants, and animals . . . and that we're all equal. But to do that, Progressives have to make you forget that your rights were endowed to you directly by your Creator, something they can best make happen by turning us all into what Progressive H. G. Wells called "enlightened Nazis"—people who look to the state for direction in every aspect of our lives, but without the violence that accompanied the Nazi movement.

But there is good news: those who are using the environment as a red herring are easy to identify. As I said earlier, people who know they are right about an issue will never back away from a debate. But that's exactly what supporters of new global warming taxes and schemes do. Sure, they write books or produce documentaries, but for an issue that could literally redefine the country, if not the world, don't we demand more than just hearing "the experts all agree"? After all, the experts once all agreed that America would never be threatened by another depression.

The Government Agrees: You Are the Problem

Gun sales are spiking. Stores are running out of ammunition. Why? Because people don't trust their government. And the feeling seems to be mutual—your government doesn't trust you, either, at least not with owning a gun.

It's not that the government is anti-gun; it's not. It purchases more guns and arms more people than any other group in America—thirty federal agencies and more than eighty-five thousand government employees or contractors carry weapons. In comparison, the entire Canadian active-duty army has fewer people carrying arms than our federal government's civilian agencies!

So, the government isn't anti-gun, but, by their constant introduction of new regulations and arduous requirements, they seem to be anti–YOU owning a gun.

The way the flawed logic in Washington apparently works is that if you're protecting federal property or providing security to government employees, our government wants to make sure you have access to a gun. But if you want that same gun to protect your family and home, our government treats you like a common criminal.

I urge you to remember that the power of government is limited to the power that we have lent it. It cannot have any power that we as citizens do not have. If government claims for itself the right to defend its property and people through the use of arms, then common sense tells us that we must also have that same right. Rights come from God to us and we lend them to government. We must never allow them to convince us that our rights come from them.

We are endowed with the right to life, liberty, and the pursuit of happiness. Again, common sense tells us that if we are so endowed we must also have the means to protect those rights. Patrick Henry summed it up like this:

> Are we at last brought to such humiliating and debasing degradation that we cannot be trusted with arms for our defense? Where is the difference between having our arms in possession and under our direction, and having them under the management of Congress? If our defense be the real object of having those arms, in whose hands can they be trusted with more propriety, or equal safety to us, as in our own hands?

There are many in Washington and in academic circles who want to leave you defenseless—they seek to compel you to rely on the government for your own protection. They believe that our best defense against gun violence is to hope that "the shooter will eventually run out of bullets." That sentiment is easily shared by those who have armed guards, send their children to private schools, and can afford to live in gated communities.

Our Second Amendment rights will continue to be under constant, yet subtle, assault. After all, politicians know better than to target the Second Amendment directly. George Mason identified this early on:

> When the resolution of enslaving America was formed in Great Britain, the British Parliament was advised by an artful man, who was governor of Pennsylvania, to disarm the people; that it was the best and most effectual way to enslave them; but that they should not do it openly, but weaken them, and let them sink gradually . . .

And that is exactly how it is happening. Consider what politicians have done or are doing to make getting, keeping, or learning about guns more difficult:

- In Washington, D.C., government officials will let you register handguns that are olive-drab green, dark earth, or black but not two-tone black because that color doesn't appear on a "safe handgun roster."
- The city of Chicago requires you to reregister your gun every year, and if you do not comply, the gun is considered "unregisterable"—meaning that it can no longer be kept within the city limits.
- In New York City, obtaining a gun permit can take nearly a year and cost more than five hundred dollars. Mountains of notarized paperwork must be meticulously filled out, including character references and driving records, and

the applicant must undergo a personal interview with a
police investigator.

There are those who will naïvely insist that these smaller
steps are necessary to promote the greater good and that our government, although not perfect, would never intentionally hurt
or imprison its own innocent citizens. They will concede that
while such actions may have taken place after guns were taken
away in Germany and the Soviet Union, such things could never
happen here. When they say this, please remind them of three
things:

1. Remind them of the victims of Presidential Executive
Order 9066, which authorized the forcible relocation of 150,000
Japanese-Americans from their homes to internment camps. This
order, signed by President Franklin Roosevelt, accepted the Progressive argument that the "greater good" required the wholesale
incarceration of Americans despite their constitutional rights
to due process and private property. Many of these Japanese-
Americans never got their homes back or property returned.

The only mistake these Japanese-Americans made was that
they believed in the rule of law and in the rights guaranteed by
our Constitution. We take most of that for granted these days, but
this black mark on our history proves that the State believes our
most basic rights can be suspended whenever it sees fit.

We see this same Progressive mind-set today playing out in
two key areas: eminent domain and privacy rights.

Eminent Domain

> ... Nor shall private property be taken for public use, without just compensation.
>
> —*Fifth Amendment, U.S. Constitution*

Eminent domain is the power of the State to take private property for what is essentially the Progressive idea of benefiting "the greater good." Historically, government was severely restricted in its ability to take your home or land. They had to have a public *use* for doing so—such as building a new highway.

The word *use* is very important and was specifically included in the Constitution's Fifth Amendment by James Madison—who also included that compensation must be provided for any property taken. Why the word *use*? It was a compromise. Our Constitution was shaped greatly by the Founders' experience with the tyrannical British government, which took private property virtually at will. Madison wanted language that he hoped would prevent our government from eventually falling into the same trap, but he had to compromise, since some Founders felt that "public *purpose*"—a term that would give the government far more power—was more appropriate.

In retrospect, arguments over purpose versus use seem irrelevant, because the Supreme Court has now weighed in. In *Kelo v. City of New London,* they sanctioned the taking of *private property* even in cases where there was no direct public use. In the *Kelo* case, it meant allowing the city to seize private property and sell it to a developer, solely for the public *benefit* of increasing the municipal tax rolls.

But "benefit" does not equal "use." A lot of things might *benefit* the greater good (such as seizing a part of town with the ugliest houses, demolishing them, and selling the land to a developer) but they're not of public *use,* so they're unconstitutional—or at least they used to be.

Private property is essential to personal freedom and liberty because it enables an individual to gain independence from the State by accumulating land, money, and wealth. In the Declaration of Independence, the Founding Fathers wanted to assert that Americans were protected in their "life, liberty and property" but were instead persuaded to write "life, liberty and the pursuit of happiness." Why? Because they didn't want southern slave states to be able to continue their practice by asserting that slaves were property and were therefore a protected right.

The importance that private property plays in preserving freedom can easily be seen in the words of those who had diametrically opposed beliefs in the role of government.

> **JOHN ADAMS:** "The moment the idea is admitted into society, that property is not as sacred as the laws of God, and that there is not a force of law and public justice to protect it, anarchy and tyranny commence."
>
> **KARL MARX:** "The theory of the Communists may be summed up in the single sentence: Abolition of private property."

Privacy Rights

It's not just our homes that are no longer secure from the whims of the State—it's also our own bodies. Almost all states now require mandatory blood-screening tests with limited opt-out provisions. The experts tell us that the testing is necessary for a host of profound medical reasons, such as protecting children. But that slippery slope is already rearing its head as efforts are now also being made to empower the State to retain, test, and research the blood and DNA of newborn babies.

I understand this can sound conspiratorial, but I do not apologize for not trusting the government to exercise caution and sound judgment. Even if their intentions are good now, who is to say what they will be in ten, twenty, or a hundred years? What limits can there possibly be on State power if it is allowed to extract a blood sample from every newborn baby without the consent of the parents?

Just as the backward idea that helping others in danger is not mandated by law, but recycling is, I believe another sign of a society in decline is when those accused of murder and rape have their blood and DNA protected more than innocent newborn babies.

2. Remind them about the tens of thousands of political, labor, and antiwar activists who were arrested for speaking out against their government and its policies beginning with Woodrow Wilson and continuing through FDR's presidency. Once again, the constitutional protections of free speech and the right to assembly meant nothing to the Progressives, who successfully argued that the "greater good" and "national security of government" were best served by arresting Americans who exercised those rights.

We see the same mind-set today—albeit on a different level. The Department of Homeland Security recently issued a report titled "Rightwing Extremism: Current Economic and Political Climate Fueling Resurgence in Radicalization and Recruitment." It essentially concludes that those who are passionate about the sanctity of life, believe in their Second Amendment right to bear arms, or are veterans of the armed forces pose a heightened security risk to the country and may require heightened monitoring. True, no one has started rounding up these "extremists" yet—but how long do you think it will be before that "national security of the government" argument is resurrected again?

There is a sad irony between the rights our leaders fight for and the ones that really matter. Remember all of those politicians who strongly objected to the wiretapping of calls between the United States and someone overseas when at least one party was *suspected* of terrorism? They couldn't believe that the government would egregiously violate the rights of Americans like that! Yet when the Department of Homeland Security says to keep an eye on tens of millions of Americans who have done nothing except obey the law and exercise their constitutional rights, these hypocrites say absolutely nothing. They truly are cockroaches who care nothing about liberty and freedom.

3. Remind them about the law-abiding citizens of New Orleans, who, while trying to protect their families and property in the wake of Hurricane Katrina, had their guns unlawfully confiscated under orders from the mayor and chief of police. This is a modern-day example of Progressive thought in action. Americans who legally purchased and owned their guns had them taken away by politicians who dismissed the Constitution and the law because it was necessary for the "greater good" and "safety of the public." And, to add insult to injury, the city of New Orleans won't try to find the rightful owners of the guns they confiscated; if they stole your gun you actually have to apply to have it returned!

And what did our elected leaders—the people who took an oath to uphold the Constitution against all enemies foreign and domestic—do after the guns of law-abiding Americans were unlawfully confiscated? They passed a law that made it illegal to take guns from law-abiding citizens. Isn't that *already* one of the protections of the Second Amendment? If the Constitution won't stop Progressives, why would passing another law?

But they had no choice. The politicians, who for decades repeatedly chastised those worried about the government confiscating guns as conspiracy theorists, got caught in their own lie. So they did what politicians do best—they tried to cover it up. They needed to deflate the fear and anger in those who realized that they'd just witnessed the Constitution being shredded, so they passed a law and said, "See, now we can't take your guns even if we want to. There's a law that stops us!"

Unfortunately, the law doesn't mean much to Progressives, because they answer to a higher moral authority. Their every action is rationalized by their belief that "the experts know best" and that their understanding of the "greater good" always trumps your individual rights. Always. When Progressives look at the Second Amendment, they don't see an individual right to bear arms, they see a collective right, under a militia, and organized by the State. While they'll rarely admit it overtly, their constant erecting of barricades to individual gun ownership indicates their real agenda.

For decades the Progressives have tried to restrict the rights of individuals to hold, possess, and use firearms, but the American people have successfully rejected most of those attempts and, fortunately, the mind-set seems to have turned against them. A 2008 Gallup Poll found that support for a handgun ban is now at its lowest level since the question was first asked . . . fifty-one years ago.

But Progressives are patient people. They move their agenda along methodically and never lose sight of where they want to take the country. The right to bear arms is the perfect example of that patience. Since Progressives can't restrict guns outright, they've tried to do an end run. In 1997, President Clinton signed a multilateral treaty called the "Inter-American Convention Against the Illicit Manufacturing of and Trafficking in Firearms, Ammunition, Explosives and other Related Materials Treaty." Why have you probably never heard of it? Because our system of checks and balances worked: the Senate never ratified the treaty.

But now, with drug violence in Mexico as the pretext, President Obama has resurrected the treaty and is urging the Senate to ratify it. Progressives like Obama don't let the law or facts slow them down in their attempts to "do good," so, during a recent visit to Mexico, the president proclaimed, "This war is being waged with guns purchased not here but in the United States. More than ninety percent of the guns recovered in Mexico come from the United States . . ."

It was a compelling statistic: 90 percent of the guns being trafficked are from the United States. QUICK—we need to do SOMETHING!

There's only one problem . . . the figure was wrong. The truth is that 90 percent of the guns that are *returned* to the United States by Mexico originally came from America—but no one knows how many guns *aren't* returned or how Mexico decides which guns to return, two important factors that skew the data. Other independent research suggests that anywhere from 17 to 36 percent of guns found at Mexican crime scenes can be traced back to the United States.

Unfortunately for those trying to promote an agenda—such as an international firearms treaty—36 percent doesn't sound nearly as convincing as 90 percent, so it's ignored.

Since President Obama and other Progressive politicians have come to power, gun and ammunition sales have soared. Is that justified? I don't know—but based on previous attempts to restrict our rights, you certainly can't fault people for being cautious. After all, what most of the "experts" in both politics and the media don't understand is that just because a gun is *bought* doesn't mean it has to be *used*. Believe it or not, exercising a right is mutually exclusive from breaking the law.

I want to propose a new American "trust indicator." When the sales of guns and bullets goes down, it means that the American people have more trust in their government. When those sales rise, it means their trust in the government to protect them and their property is falling—it's just common sense, right?

Enemies Within: Tread Carefully

Countless pages of print and hours of television time have been dedicated to covering the economic crisis, but there is something deeper and deadlier taking place that is not being reported on: an increasingly pervasive disenfranchisement among middle-class America. During the good times, Americans tolerated our politicians' malfeasance, lies, and corruption, which have weakened our families and country. But now, worsening economic conditions and a Congress filled with hypocrites are trying the patience of a restless population that has played by the rules.

If our leaders want to address the growing disdain, they need to first restore trust with the American people. If you promise that you are going to build a fence on our southern border, build a fence. If you say that you are going to clean up the government, don't appoint tax cheats to positions of power. If you promise to make America energy independent, don't refuse to discuss offshore drilling or nuclear power. If you don't know what needs to be done to fix our economic meltdown, don't spend trillions of dollars, take control of private companies, vilify corporate executives, and tell us that everything will be okay.

Common sense tells us that the public will lose its faith in any government where 66 percent of the people have absolutely "no trust" or "not very much trust" in the government's ability to manage its "finances reasonably." Logic tells us that when only 22 percent of a citizenry trusts the government to do what's right "most of the time," something has to give.

But the Progressives won't "give" because they, along with their useful idiots, don't think like you. They are part of the 7 percent of Americans that a Rasmussen survey recently defined as the "political class" who:

- trust the judgment of political leaders more than the American public;
- reject the notion that government is a special-interest group primarily watching out for itself;
- believe that big business and big government *work together* for the interests of investors and consumers.

Given the beliefs of that group, is it any wonder that while 51 percent of all Americans have a "favorable" view of the nationwide Tea Parties, and another 32 percent have a "very favorable" view—a full 81 percent of people who identify themselves as part of the "political class" have either an "unfavorable" or "highly unfavorable" view?

They just don't see the world the same way, and they are working to make sure that you and your children succumb to their views. You feel they are talking down to you—and you feel that way because *they are* talking down to you! They not only believe that they *have* the answer (bigger government) but that theirs is also the *only* answer.

If you feel the condescension of the political and media elite, you have Walter Lippmann to thank. Mr. Lippmann was a highly influential journalist and Progressive during the Wilson and Roosevelt administrations who argued that the media should play a role as intermediary between politicians and a public too self-centered and uneducated to really grasp what was really going on. He was noted to have remarked that most people were "mentally children or barbarians" and needed self-anointed experts to help them navigate through the issues and decisions they would be called upon as citizens to make.

Every time you hear a politician explain a vote to the American public by saying "this was a very complex issue" or "this was a nuanced bill" and then skip the part where they *explain* that alleged complexity or nuance, you are seeing a living example of Lippmann's philosophy. It's the politicians' politically correct way of telling you that "you just wouldn't understand."

By dismissing the average American as uninterested in the issues, or not smart enough to understand them, the political class is breeding disenfranchisement and resentment. The only way out is by restoring America's confidence. We need leaders who will say what they mean and mean what they say. Leaders who will tell the American people what their convictions are, not what they think we want to hear. Honesty may not sound great in cable news sound bites, but it will sound great to the millions of people who've been craving it. We will have your back.

Vermont's Senator Bernie Sanders is a self-described socialist. He doesn't hide from his views and he makes no apologies for his policies. For that, I respect him deeply. I would much rather have a country filled with honest brokers whose policies I abhor than one filled with people who say what I want to hear, but then do exactly the opposite. Being honest about your principles means that there can be a real debate on the issues, with the chance of real progress being made.

It's not just the political class who has mastered the art of deception. There are other potentially deadly masters who will seek to exploit your frustration and sense of desperation. Many will warn you of government tyranny; they'll talk of secret societies, vast conspiracies, shadow governments, and the need for violent action. I urge you to stay away from these individuals and those ideas.

There is no "star chamber" that needs to be found and destroyed, and there is no global conspiracy playing out. The individuals and groups that propagate those lies have their own agendas, but, like all radicals and revolutionaries, they will eventually seek to impose their rules and lifestyle on all of us.

Make no mistake, a revolution *is* required to restore America, but it's a revolution that can be fought with the weapons of democracy. This is not a call to arms or violence—it is a call to once again tether ourselves to our core principles and values. Treachery and treason abound from those who profess allegiance to America. Truth, the "first casualty in war," is in short supply—make it your polestar.

Objective reason and innate common sense tell us that loyalty to government either comes voluntarily due to the respect its citizens give it for a job well done, or involuntarily through threats of force or outright fear. The polling data discussed earlier makes it clear that our government is quickly moving toward the latter. That is an unsustainable shift.

Like our parents and grandparents, most of us grew up in an era when our schools sought to instill confidence and respect in our government and its leaders. We learned of the selflessness of George Washington, the honesty of Abraham Lincoln, and the sacrifice Americans made to turn a group of thirteen colonies into the United States. We learned how our country came together to crush Nazism and fascism and put a man on the moon. The knowledge of those events, and our government's proud role in them, inspired generation after generation of Americans.

But we are losing the next generation to an educational system that has fallen prey to political patronage and the Progressive agenda. History, reading, writing, and math are secondary to the incessant indoctrination of our kids to climate change, the evils of capitalism, and the benefits of big government. This works as a general anesthesia, numbing our children and rendering them defenseless to the lessons and ideas that we work so hard to inoculate them from in our own homes.

Given the importance of education in shaping the future of America, it's not surprising that it has been a main target of the Progressive movement's agenda. During the early 1900s, Progressives increased the mandatory nature of education, which resulted in enrollment for elementary and high school age children going up, right along with public school spending. But getting more kids into the classrooms didn't matter unless Progressives could also influence what was being taught in those classrooms.

Woodrow Wilson, then the president of Princeton University, candidly explained, "Our problem is not merely to help the students to adjust themselves to world life . . . [but] to make them as unlike their fathers as we can."

Progressives didn't want learning to be from teachers to students, they wanted it to be based on the children's own experiences and feelings. They wanted to develop a structure where children were "equal participants" with their teachers in a classroom community. But it hasn't worked. Consider that:

- Only 34.6 percent of the kids in Baltimore city's public school system received a high school diploma in 2004;
- The Indianapolis public school system handed out diplomas to just 30.5 percent of its students;
- Detroit's public school system struggled to have 25 percent of its students qualify for a high school diploma;
- 45.2 percent of New York City public school kids graduated with a high school diploma.

Yet, despite those sobering statistics, Progressives still don't view parents as partners in the learning cycle—they view them as obstacles. Parents, with their rigid views of test scores and report cards, hold their children back from realizing their full potential, value, and role in the greater community. And, once again, we find parallels to that kind of thinking in history.

In the 1700s, French revolutionary Maximilien Robespierre wanted all children to be nurtured and taught by the state. In the 1900s, Hitler told his supporters that those opposing the Third Reich and its ideologies were destined to fail because, as he put it, "Your child belongs to us already," and that child will only grow up to know the "new camp" in which he is being raised.

More recently, Hillary Clinton (who once said "I consider myself a modern progressive") pronounced that it "takes a village" to raise a child, suggesting that the community has a vested interest in deciding what each child is taught and how he or she is raised. Clinton and other Progressives truly believe that "there isn't really any such thing as someone else's child."

Because so much of what the Progressives stand for *feels good*, it wasn't a hard sell to educators and sociologist experts. They bought into the "classroom community" concept and urged our teachers to act as "friends" to children. As a result, kids have been taught for years that they are all equals in the classroom and that feelings matter more than test scores. As those kids make their way into the workforce, we will see those new ideals influence American business. If competitiveness and hard work never mattered in the classroom, it won't matter in their jobs, either.

But even as these policies degrade America's standing in the world, Progressives are still pushing forward. It's not enough to have moved educational responsibility from the local community to the state to the federal government—they now want to move it to the global level.

The United Nations Convention on the Rights of the Child, which has been ratified by every U.N. member except the United States and Somalia, requires that countries give children certain "rights," including: access to education and health care; programs that develop their personalities and talents; and the opportunity to grow and develop in an atmosphere of peace, dignity, tolerance, freedom, equality, and solidarity.

As the treaty itself says, "By agreeing to undertake the obligations of the Convention [by ratifying or acceding to it], national governments have committed themselves to protecting and ensuring children's rights and they have agreed to hold themselves accountable for this commitment before the international community."

Answering to the "international community" is exactly where the Progressives have been trying to push us and it's why there are once again calls in Congress for the United States to adopt this convention. Just as was the case after we refused to ratify the Kyoto Treaty, we are told that America is out of step with the rest of a world that is "progressing" while we stick to our "outdated" principles.

The truth is that all of these attempts to "take care of your children" are nothing more than an effort to break down the cohesion and structure of the parent/child relationship while also migrating power to a national or global entity. The Progressives recognize that family is the basic, most fundamental building block of society and they realize that by degrading the power of the parents, they are establishing, in the minds of children, the power and "compassion" of the State.

Examples of this can already be found. Your child doesn't have to tell you when they are using school-distributed contraceptives, seeing a school nurse, or even scheduling an abortion. The parents are effectively left out of these life-changing and emotionally demanding decisions as the State happily steps in as their surrogate.

For those who continue to fight and resist, the government is watching. It doesn't matter if common sense, or even facts, are on your side—if something goes against the Progressive agenda, it will be targeted. Consider the Washington, D.C., school voucher program, for instance. It didn't matter to the political elite and their union allies that the kids using that program were scoring substantially higher than their public school counterparts, or that 8,000 students desperate to escape the public schools applied for just 1,714 scholarships, or that the $7,500 voucher provided cost half as much as the district would pay for that same child to attend a public school. It didn't matter because charter schools put a wall between government and education—and that wall cannot stand . . . so neither could the D.C. voucher program.

Despite a swelling budget that seemed to fund every possible program, the Obama administration killed the voucher program by refusing to allow any new children into it. It is expected that the program will die a slow, silent death. In the eyes of the education "experts," it's better that children attend failing, miserable, unsafe public schools overseen by the government, than have a chance at something better in a facility with less government control. Such is the power and contempt of our leaders.

Homeschooling is another area that Progressives target simply because the government does not get a seat at the kitchen table. Progressives label those who homeschool their children as "backwards," "socially undeveloped," or religious zealots—but those attacks are just diversions from their real concern about lack of State control.

You may scoff and figure that homeschooling attacks, like infringements on the right to bear arms, will never succeed—but you're wrong. It was just a few years ago that a California appellate court found that "parents do not have a constitutional right to home-school their children" under California law. The basis for their decision: "A primary purpose of the educational system is to train schoolchildren in good citizenship, patriotism and loyalty to the state and the nation as a means of protecting the public welfare." Apparently the court determined that patriotism and loyalty to "the state" couldn't be guaranteed in a home setting.

Many will counter that this decision was reversed and that homeschooling is alive and well in California today. While that may be true, I would remind you that Progressive policy makers are patient. They know how to bide their time, waiting for the right combination of public opinion and judicial appointees to take hold before making their case again. And if that fails, they will move their battle to the international level by seeking to have their version of what's best for your children dictated by the United Nations through treaties such as the "Convention on the Rights of the Child."

Progressives do not care about minor setbacks. They will continue their assault because they do not fear us. And, truthfully, they have no reason to. We have failed to stand up to them time and time again even as they've worked tirelessly and openly to restructure and reshape America.

Common sense tells you that if the government was willing to bring its power and might to prevent another 1,700 poor children from getting a school voucher in Washington, D.C., they'll work even harder to bring a million homeschooled children into the public schools so that "loyalty to the state and the nation as a means of protecting the public welfare" can be taught appropriately.

For too long we've believed the idea sold to us by politicians and bureaucrats that money is the answer to the problems with our education system. It's not—the answer is in standing against the Progressive policies that have led us to this destruction. We don't need more money, we just need more teachers who care, more politicians who are willing to do the right thing, more parents who are willing to fight for a return to the traditional parent/ teacher relationship, and most of all, *fewer* professional bureaucrats standing in the way of commonsense reform.

Only a Moral and Religious People

The false idea that money can solve any problem isn't confined to education. We all started to believe that notion. If we didn't have the money, we acted like we did. We felt like we deserved to have it all—big homes, big cars, big TVs. Even as our families became smaller, our homes got bigger, with the average home size growing from 983 square feet in 1950 to 2,512 square feet today. Naturally, those bigger homes came with a bigger price tag. The median home price went from $65,087 (adjusted for inflation) to $165,400 over that same fifty-eight-year period.

It's a sad contradiction, but our homes now seem to have plenty of room for everything—except God. New technology makes us more efficient at work, but we spend less time with our children. The Internet has made the world smaller, yet we're more disconnected from our communities than ever before.

Yet, despite it all, we eagerly line up for more!

Tennis great Arthur Ashe described what happened to our communities back during the Los Angeles riots in 1992. "I felt sick," he said. "That's not us . . . We were once a people of dignity and morality; we wanted the world to be fair to us, and we tried, on the whole, to be fair to the world. Now I was looking at a new order that is based squarely on revenge, not justice, with morality discarded. Instead of settling on what's right, or just, or moral, the idea is to get even."

The truth that many people are now learning the hard way is that money isn't the solution to our problems—*we are*. Good families require good parents. Good communities require good neighbors. And good government requires good citizens.

We have always been a nation who selflessly sacrifices for our families, our communities, and our country. But today we are experiencing a change in what it means to be a volunteer.

Under President Obama, the AmeriCorps program purports to be a volunteer organization dedicated to service. Each participant, however, is paid a monthly stipend adding up to several thousands of dollars annually. Service also comes with an "award" that helps defray the cost of college, another benefit worth thousands of dollars annually. Common sense tells us that if you're paid for your work you're an employee or a contractor, not a volunteer.

While this subtle change may seem harmless, it reflects the Progressive mind-set that it's more important to get the youth involved in the AmeriCorps program than it is for them to experience the selflessness that actual volunteer work is all about. The reason is that Progressives are trying to redefine service, volunteerism, and charity in an attempt to further combine the secular with the spiritual. They want to erase any barrier between government-sanctioned *work* and government-sanctioned *volunteerism*. To them it's all one and the same.

At this time of great need for values such as goodness, virtue, and modesty, religion is increasingly being targeted as the barrier instead of being embraced as a savior. This lie needs to be rejected—not by words, but by example. Religion is not the cause of intolerance any more than the lack of it is the cause of mass murder. People are responsible for their own behavior—those who kill in the name of any religion are just as delusional as those who, like Stalin and Hitler, kill for no one but themselves.

So why is religion so important to the proper functioning of a democracy? Well, once again, our Founding Fathers had the answer. In a letter to the president of Yale University, Benjamin Franklin once wrote:

> Here is my creed: I believe in one God, the Creator of the universe. That he governs it by his providence. That he ought to be worshipped. That the most acceptable service we render to him is in doing good to his other children. That the soul of man is immortal, and will be treated with justice in another life respecting its conduct in this. These I take to be the fundamental points in all sound religion.

It wasn't about any one particular creed, dogma, or church, but rather about all religions that inspired men to selflessness, virtue, and godliness. Our Founders understood the thing that we try so hard to forget today: there is far more that unites us than divides us. Virtue, honesty, and character aren't the purview of any particular congregation; they can be found in any church that has God as its foundation. We have forgotten this lesson and instead of using religion as our anchor, we use it to shame or blame. To many in this country, those who attend church regularly aren't pillars of their community, they're freaks or extremists.

But that mind-set can be changed by setting an example of tolerance and unparalleled acceptance toward each other. Let's stop using our religious symbols to score political points. Are we that insecure in our own faith that the religious symbols or public prayers of a different religion cannot be welcomed with open arms? As Thomas Jefferson once said:

> Question with boldness even the existence of a God; because, if there be one, he must more approve of the homage of reason,

than that of blind-folded fear . . . Do not be frightened from this inquiry from any fear of its consequences. If it ends in the belief that there is no God, you will find incitements to virtue in the comfort and pleasantness you feel in its exercise . . .

Religions and their followers must stop turning on each other. We are a land founded through divine Providence, a land where, as James Madison said, the "spirit of liberty and patriotism animates all degrees and denominations of men."

But Progressives don't see it that way. They want us at each other's throats because a house divided cannot stand *against them*. They recognize that religion is a unifying force and a counterbalance to state power, so they believe that it must either be harnessed by the state or destroyed. There cannot be a rival for American's allegiance.

As with the other issues we've covered, Progressives recognize that they cannot change this overnight. They understand the powerful role that religion plays and so they won't come out and directly repudiate it. Instead, they will seek to co-opt its doctrines where they can, much as Woodrow Wilson did when he pronounced, "There is no higher religion than human service. To work for the common good is the greatest creed." His Republican predecessor, Theodore Roosevelt, claimed that when the people voted on who should be their president, the process should "be treated as next to the voice of God."

By substituting the "common good" for God as the highest form of religion, they are subtly saying that your rights, freedoms, and liberties come from *government* instead of, as the Founding Fathers taught, directly from God, and that you *lend* some of those rights to government.

French Progressive Jean-Jacques Rousseau argued that religion and politics should be aligned in their goals and aspirations for the community. Allegiance to one should automatically trigger allegiance to the other.

But it's more than simply invoking the name of God or religion; it is the devout belief that the work of government is *furthering* the work of God. The concept of a "social gospel" is not something reserved for history. At this year's National Prayer Breakfast, President Obama shared that his religious conversion took place while doing community organizing work on the streets of Chicago. There's nothing wrong with that, but it shows that, for Obama, community organizing wasn't just a political endeavor, it was a spiritual one as well. So when Obama then called for Americans "to treat with dignity and respect those with whom we share a brief moment on this Earth," something he called the "Golden Rule"—it's likely that he looks at it as his duty to use the levers and power of government to make that happen.

Evidence of that belief can be found in how our leaders look at charitable giving. Despite a six-figure salary, Vice President Joe Biden has given an average of $369 to charity each year for the last decade. Before considering a run for president, Barack Obama donated about 1 percent of his salary to charity. I am not a person who will ever tell others how or where to spend their money, but given the Progressive priorities, and the way President Obama views AmeriCorps, I doubt that this reflects stinginess. Instead, it likely reflects their belief that charitable giving is secondary to charitable action, something that they fulfill by promoting a "greater good" agenda.

We must not fall into that trap and we must not become the hypocrites that our politicians already are. We cannot preach tolerance and then practice the opposite. Franklin once observed that "only a virtuous people are capable of freedom." That's because democracy requires self-regulation, a virtue that those who practice greed and hate are incapable of mastering. But the cause of freedom is too important to let those who are incapable of self-sufficiency destroy it. Remember, to us, slavery and tyranny are far-fetched concepts that history has righted—but to *history*, the far-fetched concept is the idea that men should be free.

VI

IS IT A RISING
OR A SETTING SUN?

The time has come for a second American Revolution—bring your passion, but leave your muskets at home. This revolution will take place in our minds and hearts. Instead of liberating us from a tyrannical monarchy, it will liberate us from our own tyrannical thinking.

This revolution will be won when enough Americans rebel against the lies that are being told by those in power, lies such as the idea that we can't look at the past to learn about the future, that our founding principles are outdated, or that only those in power know what's best.

The tangible result of this rebellion, the way you can *show everyone* that you are serious, is to leave whatever political party you currently belong to. Stop donating to the faceless RNC or DNC and starting devoting your time, energy, and, if appropriate, your dollars to the *people* who stand for your values.

When that begins to happen, the two parties will start to panic. Independent thinkers will become the biggest special-interest group in America, and the establishment will *fear you*.

That is why they must keep us fighting each other—fear and anger are their only defense against the citizenry educating themselves enough to see through their lies and corruption.

There is a reason why it was illegal to teach a slave to read. Slaveowners knew then what our two-party system knows now: an educated man will throw off the chains of bondage and demand to rule himself.

Those in Washington believe that there are many sheep and no shepherds. So we must let them know in the most unequivocal of terms: WE ARE NOT SHEEP. AMERICANS HAVE NEVER BEEN SHEEP. We are shepherds—and if we don't soon reclaim our rightful place at the head of the flock, we will lose it forever.

There are some who call for violent revolution. They are wrong. Our future does not lie down that bloody path. Once that spirit is released, it is uncontrollable, and, I assure you, we will be worse off as individuals, communities, and country if we let others attempt to take us down that well-traveled road.

Weapons and violence are easier to overcome than the truth. The established powers can win a war of bullets, but they cannot win a war against passionate ideas, a war fought based on the rule of law, or a war rooted in values reflected by our founding documents.

With that being said, make no mistake, NOW IS THE TIME. This *is* a call for action. Stand and link arm in arm. Our nation is being redefined right in front of our eyes; it is time we have a say in what it will look like. We must draw a line in the sand and let our voices be heard loud and clear:

Don't Tread on Me.

This task is not small or for the faint of heart. While lives will not be lost, they will be destroyed and reputations will forever be tarnished. And that's okay; it's a small price to pay for victory, as history has shown that if we lose our grasp on freedom, it will likely never be enjoyed by us again. If the American experiment fails, then so does the cause of liberty—not just here, but around the world.

One day we will face our children and grandchildren as they ask us what we found more important and valuable than freedom. They will ask if our big, unaffordable homes, "free" universal health care, and "buy it now" lifestyle were worth enslaving them for.

How will you answer?

Just as we look back with pride and awe at what the generations before us did to preserve the cause of freedom, our children and grandchildren will look back at us. But should we now fail, it won't be with pride or awe, it will be with disgust. As they toil under oppressive taxes and tyrannical rule, they will continually question what we were so busy doing that we did not notice the stripping away of our freedoms and liberties. As they are forced to carry the yoke of servitude imposed by their domestic and foreign masters they will question why we did nothing. *Did you not see it coming?* they'll wonder.

The choice is ours: Do we continue to lie to ourselves now or tell our children lies later?

Our freedom, liberty, and continued transformation into a better place will not come from the politicians in Washington or from the United Nations, the G-20, the IMF, or any other organization. It will only come from us. Each of us stands as a sentinel against oppression, just as our ancestors have for twenty generations. There will be temporal as well as eternal consequences for each of us should we abandon our post and let liberty's light slip away into the darkness.

I said at the beginning that I think I know who you are—but

that's only because I know who I am. We may not agree on everything, but we both know that what is now happening does not feel right.

No one told us to be good to each other on 9/12, it just happened.

We know that our best days aren't behind us. We know that America is the country that freed millions of people in the last hundred years alone. We are the people who changed the world.

America's promise of freedom allowed the lone entrepreneur to bring the world the lightbulb, car, telephone, movie, assembly line, artificial heart, computer, bifocals, sewing machine, refrigerator, air conditioner, safety pin, television, cash register, crayon, power tools, the oil well, water tower, Popsicle, blue jeans, elevator, repeating rifle, laser, polio vaccine, microwave oven, copy machine, fiber optics, and cotton candy.

We are only a simple change of mind-set from being that nation again. As we found out on September 12, miracles only require a change in perspective.

When we stop telling ourselves we can't do it or that our best days are behind us things will begin to change. Start telling yourself, "I don't need the government to do it for me." Stop being a slave and you will start seeing miracles.

The first step in recovery is to admit you have a problem. So say it. Say it out loud, "We have a problem." Admit your role in it—maybe it's "I spent too much," "I didn't pay attention at the polls," "I played partisan politics," "I was too afraid or tired to get involved," "I was too slow to remember my values and my principles," or "I rationalized the decisions and choices I made."

It doesn't matter. Leave the past in the past and seize the future. That shining city on the hill is still there.

Make no mistake, the actions you must take are simple in language, but complex in practice. They will demand your time, your attention, and your resolve. Have patience, but also carry a sense of urgency—the clock is ticking.

Assemble with passion, peace, and power, and march on Washington. Let your voice be heard and your anger be seen. Some will label your words as inciting or dangerous; help them understand that the truth will always sound angry to those who can't recognize it.

DO NOT WAIT FOR OTHERS TO SAY AND DO THE THINGS YOU FEEL. The American Republic will not be swept into the dustbin of history if good men come forward now. Rest assured that others more timid than you will join in the fight, but they wait for you.

Stand shoulder to shoulder and arm in arm unafraid. Listen, learn, and lead. Renew that promise first made during a hot summer in Philadelphia and mutually pledge to each other our lives, our fortunes, and our sacred honor.

After the signing of the Constitution in 1787, Benjamin Franklin spoke about a chair belonging to General Washington. At the top of the chair were the golden rays of the sun. He told Washington that throughout all of the proceedings he had wondered if it was a rising or a setting sun.

When Washington asked him, "What have you decided, Mr. Franklin?" he did not hesitate with his response.

"It is a rising sun."

I believe that is still true today. Great and powerful miracles are about to unfold before us—but only if we decide right here and right now that our sun is still rising. Once we do that, once we dedicate ourselves to that new dawn and experience a restoration of our founding principles, we can be secure in the knowledge that future generations will enjoy the same liberties and freedoms that were reserved for us.

But until then, the sense that something just doesn't feel right will linger.

> ... until an independence is declared, the Continent will feel itself like a man who continues putting off some unpleasant business from day to day, yet knows it must be done, hates to set about it, wishes it over, and is continually haunted with the thoughts of its necessity.

Those are the last words of Thomas Paine's call to action— and so they become the last words of mine as well. Under normal circumstances, words like those have no meaning or influence unless people give them power.

But these are not normal circumstances and those words are not just words. Those words find their roots in an idea that seems to have been all but abandoned . . .

. . . Common Sense.

THE 9.12 PROJECT

Visit the912project.com for more information

The 9 Principles:

1. America is good.
2. I believe in God and He is the Center of my Life.
3. I must always try to be a more honest person than I was yesterday.
4. The family is sacred. My spouse and I are the ultimate authority, not the government.
5. If you break the law you pay the penalty. Justice is blind and no one is above it.
6. I have a right to life, liberty, and the pursuit of happiness, but there is no guarantee of equal results.
7. I work hard for what I have and I will share it with who I want to. Government cannot force me to be charitable.
8. It is not un-American for me to disagree with authority or to share my personal opinion.
9. The government works for me. I do not answer to them; they answer to me.

The 12 Values:

Honesty	Sincerity
Reverence	Moderation
Hope	Hard Work
Thrift	Courage
Humility	Personal Responsibility
Charity	Gratitude

Let Your Journey Begin Here

I hope this book serves as a solid starting point in your journey to learn more about your country, its history, and what needs to be done to put her back on course.

But this book can be only that: a starting point. You must continue your education and learning so that you will recognize those people whose plans and policies promote personal freedom and responsibility, along with the danger signs of those whose policies will do the opposite.

These books are just a few that I have read over the past twelve months that have really opened my eyes. I believe the first two should be required reading. *The 5000 Year Leap* is essential to understanding why our Founders built this Republic the way they did, and *American Progressivism* will reveal how the country began to leave its core roots and where that pathway ultimately leads.

Additional Reading

The 5000 Year Leap: A Miracle That Changed the World, by W. Cleon Skousen (National Center for Constitutional Studies)

American Progressivism, edited by Ronald J. Pestritto and William J. Atto (Lexington)

The Real Benjamin Franklin, by Andrew M. Allison, M. Richard Maxfield, and W. Cleon Skousen (National Center for Constitutional Studies)

The Forgotten Man: A New History of the Great Depression, by Amity Shlaes (HarperCollins)

The Real George Washington, by Andrew M. Allison, Jay A. Parry, and W. Cleon Skousen (National Center for Constitutional Studies)

Lenin, Stalin, and Hitler: The Age of Social Catastrophe, by Robert Gellately (Vintage)

Liberal Fascism: The Secret History of the American Left, from Mussolini to the Politics of Meaning, by Jonah Goldberg (Doubleday)

New Deal or Raw Deal? How FDR's Economic Legacy Has Damaged America, by Burton Folsom, Jr. (Threshold Editions)

The Real Thomas Jefferson, by Andrew M. Allison, K. DeLynn Cook, M. Richard Maxfield, and W. Cleon Skousen (National Center for Constitutional Studies)

Woodrow Wilson and the Roots of Modern Liberalism, by Ronald J. Pestritto (Rowman & Littlefield)

THOMAS PAINE'S

COMMON SENSE

INTRODUCTION

Perhaps the sentiments contained in the following pages, are not yet sufficiently fashionable to procure them general favor; a long habit of not thinking a thing wrong, gives it a superficial appearance of being right, and raises at first a formidable outcry in defence of custom. But tumult soon subsides. Time makes more converts than reason.

As a long and violent abuse of power is generally the means of calling the right of it in question, (and in matters too which might never have been thought of, had not the sufferers been aggravated into the inquiry,) and as the king of England hath undertaken in his own right, to support the parliament in what he calls theirs, and as the good people of this country are grievously oppressed by the combination, they have an undoubted privilege to inquire into the pretensions of both, and equally to reject the usurpations of either.

In the following sheets, the author hath studiously avoided every thing which is personal among ourselves. Compliments as well as censure to individuals make no part thereof. The wise and the worthy need not the triumph of a pamphlet; and those whose sentiments are injudicious or unfriendly, will cease of themselves, unless too much pains are bestowed upon their conversion.

The cause of America is, in a great measure, the cause of all mankind. Many circumstances have, and will arise, which are not local, but universal, and through which the principles of all lovers of mankind are affected, and in the event of which, their affections are interested. The laying a country desolate with fire and sword, declaring war against the natural rights of all mankind, and extirpating the defenders thereof from the face of the earth, is the concern of every man to whom nature hath given the power of feeling; of which class, regardless of party censure, is

The Author.

Philadelphia, Feb. 14, 1776.

OF THE ORIGIN AND DESIGN OF GOVERNMENT IN GENERAL, WITH CONCISE REMARKS ON THE ENGLISH CONSTITUTION

S ome writers have so confounded society with government, as to leave little or no distinction between them; whereas they are not only different, but have different origins. Society is produced by our wants, and government by our wickedness; the former promotes our happiness positively by uniting our affections, the latter negatively by restraining our vices. The one encourages intercourse, the other creates distinctions. The first is a patron, the last a punisher.

Society in every state is a blessing, but government even in its best state is but a necessary evil; in its worst state an intolerable one; for when we suffer, or are exposed to the same miseries by a government, which we might expect in a country without government, our calamity is heightened by reflecting that we furnish the means by which we suffer! Government, like dress, is the badge of lost innocence; the palaces of kings are built on the ruins of the bowers of paradise. For were the impulses of conscience clear, uniform, and irresistibly obeyed, man would need no other lawgiver; but that not being the case, he finds it necessary to surrender up a part of his property to furnish means for the protection of the rest; and this he is induced to do by the same prudence which in every other case advises him out of two evils to choose the least. Wherefore, security being the true design and end of government, it unanswerably follows that whatever form thereof appears most likely to ensure it to us, with the least expense and greatest benefit, is preferable to all others.

In order to gain a clear and just idea of the design and end of government, let us suppose a small number of persons settled in some sequestered part of the earth, unconnected with the rest, they will then represent the first peopling of any country, or of the world. In this state of natural liberty, society will be their first thought. A thousand motives will excite them thereto, the strength of one man is so unequal to his wants, and his mind so unfitted for perpetual solitude, that he is soon obliged to seek assistance and relief of another, who in his turn requires the same. Four or five united would be able to raise a tolerable dwelling in the midst of a wilderness, but one man might labor out the common period of life without accomplishing any thing; when he had felled his timber he could not remove it, nor erect it after it was removed; hunger in the mean time would urge him from his work, and every different want call him a different way. Disease, nay even misfortune would be death, for though neither might be mortal, yet either would disable him from living, and reduce him to a state in which he might rather be said to perish than to die.

Thus necessity, like a gravitating power, would soon form our newly arrived emigrants into society, the reciprocal blessings of which, would supersede, and render the obligations of law and government unnecessary while they remained perfectly just to each other; but as nothing but heaven is impregnable to vice, it will unavoidably happen, that in proportion as they surmount the first difficulties of emigration, which bound them together in a common cause, they will begin to relax in their duty and attachment to each other; and this remissness will point out the necessity, of establishing some form of government to supply the defect of moral virtue.

Some convenient tree will afford them a State-House, under the branches of which, the whole colony may assemble to deliberate on public matters. It is more than probable that their first laws will have the title only of Regulations, and be enforced by no other penalty than public disesteem. In this first parliament every man, by natural right, will have a seat.

But as the colony increases, the public concerns will increase likewise, and the distance at which the members may be separated, will render it too inconvenient for all of them to meet on every occasion as at first, when their number was small, their habitations near, and the public concerns few and trifling. This will point out the convenience of their consenting to leave the legislative part to be managed by a select number chosen from the whole body, who are supposed to have the same concerns at stake which those have who appointed them, and who will act in the same manner as the whole body would act, were they present. If the colony continues increasing, it will become necessary to augment the number of the representatives, and that the interest of every part of the colony may be attended to, it will be found best to divide the whole into convenient parts, each part sending its proper number; and that the elected might never form to themselves an interest separate from the electors, prudence will point out the propriety of having elections often; because as the elected might by that means return and mix again with the general body of the electors in a few months, their fidelity to the public will be secured by the prudent reflection of not making a rod for themselves. And as this frequent interchange will establish a common interest with every part of the community, they will mutually and naturally support each other, and on this (not on the unmeaning name of king) depends the strength of government, and the happiness of the governed.

Here then is the origin and rise of government; namely, a mode rendered necessary by the inability of moral virtue to govern the world; here too is the design and end of government, viz., freedom and security. And however our eyes may be dazzled with show, or our ears deceived by sound; however prejudice may warp our wills, or interest darken our understanding, the simple voice of nature and of reason will say, it is right.

I draw my idea of the form of government from a principle in nature, which no art can overturn, viz., that the more simple any thing is, the less liable it is to be disordered, and the easier repaired when disordered; and with this maxim in view, I offer a few remarks on the so much boasted constitution of England. That it was noble for the dark and slavish times in which it was erected is granted. When the world was overrun with tyranny the least remove therefrom was a glorious rescue. But that it is imperfect, subject to convulsions, and incapable of producing what it seems to promise, is easily demonstrated.

Absolute governments (though the disgrace of human nature) have this advantage with them, that they are simple; if the people suffer, they know the head from which their suffering springs, know likewise the remedy, and are not bewildered by a variety of causes and cures. But the constitution of England is so exceedingly complex, that the nation may suffer for years together without being able to discover in which part the fault lies, some will say in one and some in another, and every political physician will advise a different medicine.

I know it is difficult to get over local or long standing prejudices, yet if we will suffer ourselves to examine the component parts of the English constitution, we shall find them to be the base remains of two ancient tyrannies, compounded with some new republican materials.

First.—The remains of monarchical tyranny in the person of the king. Secondly.—The remains of aristocratical tyranny in the persons of the peers. Thirdly.—The new republican materials in the persons of the commons, on whose virtue depends the freedom of England.

The two first, by being hereditary, are independent of the people; wherefore in a constitutional sense they contribute nothing towards the freedom of the state.

To say that the constitution of England is a union of three powers reciprocally checking each other, is farcical, either the words have no meaning, or they are flat contradictions.

To say that the commons is a check upon the king, presupposes two things.

First.—That the king is not to be trusted without being looked after, or in other words, that a thirst for absolute power is the natural disease of monarchy. Secondly.—That the commons, by being appointed for that purpose, are either wiser or more worthy of confidence than the crown.

But as the same constitution which gives the commons a power to check the king by withholding the supplies, gives afterwards the king a power to check the commons, by empowering him to reject their other bills; it again supposes that the king is wiser than those whom it has already supposed to be wiser than him. A mere absurdity!

There is something exceedingly ridiculous in the composition of monarchy; it first excludes a man from the means of information, yet empowers him to act in cases where the highest judgment is required. The state of a king shuts him from the world, yet the business of a king requires him to know it thoroughly; wherefore the different parts, unnaturally opposing and destroying each other, prove the whole character to be absurd and useless.

Some writers have explained the English constitution thus; the king, say they, is one, the people another; the peers are an house in behalf of the king; the commons in behalf of the people; but this hath all the distinctions of an house divided against itself; and though the expressions be pleasantly arranged, yet when examined they appear idle and ambiguous; and it will always happen, that the nicest construction that words are capable of, when applied to the description of something which either cannot exist, or is too incomprehensible to be within the compass of description, will be words of sound only, and though they may amuse the ear, they cannot inform the mind, for this explanation includes a previous question, viz., How came the king by a power which the people are afraid to trust, and always obliged to check? Such a power could not be the gift of a wise people, neither can any power, which needs checking, be from God; yet the provision, which the constitution makes, supposes such a power to exist.

But the provision is unequal to the task; the means either cannot or will not accomplish the end, and the whole affair is a felo de se; for as the greater weight will always carry up the less, and as all the wheels of a machine are put in motion by one, it only remains to know which power in the constitution has the most weight, for that will govern; and though the others, or a part of them, may clog, or, as the phrase is, check the rapidity of its motion, yet so long as they cannot stop it, their endeavors will be ineffectual; the first moving power will at last have its way, and what it wants in speed is supplied by time.

That the crown is this overbearing part in the English constitution needs not be mentioned, and that it derives its whole consequence merely from being the giver of places and pensions is self-evident, wherefore, though we have been wise enough to shut and lock a door against absolute monarchy, we at the same time have been foolish enough to put the crown in possession of the key.

The prejudice of Englishmen, in favor of their own government by king, lords, and commons, arises as much or more from national pride than reason. Individuals are undoubtedly safer in England than in some other countries, but the will of the king is as much the law of the land in Britain as in France, with this difference, that instead of proceeding directly from his mouth, it is handed to the people under the most formidable shape of an act of parliament. For the fate of Charles the First hath only made kings more subtle—not more just.

Wherefore, laying aside all national pride and prejudice in favor of modes and forms, the plain truth is, that it is wholly owing to the constitution of the people, and not to the constitution of the government, that the crown is not as oppressive in England as in Turkey.

An inquiry into the constitutional errors in the English form of government is at this time highly necessary; for as we are never in a proper condition of doing justice to others, while we continue under the influence of some leading partiality, so neither are we capable of doing it to ourselves while we remain fettered by any obstinate prejudice. And as a man, who is attached to a prostitute, is unfitted to choose or judge of a wife, so any prepossession in favor of a rotten constitution of government will disable us from discerning a good one.

OF MONARCHY
AND HEREDITARY
SUCCESSION

Mankind being originally equals in the order of creation, the equality could only be destroyed by some subsequent circumstance; the distinctions of rich, and poor, may in a great measure be accounted for, and that without having recourse to the harsh, ill-sounding names of oppression and avarice. Oppression is often the consequence, but seldom or never the means of riches; and though avarice will preserve a man from being necessitously poor, it generally makes him too timorous to be wealthy.

But there is another and greater distinction for which no truly natural or religious reason can be assigned, and that is, the distinction of men into KINGS and SUBJECTS. Male and female are the distinctions of nature, good and bad the distinctions of heaven; but how a race of men came into the world so exalted above the rest, and distinguished like some new species, is worth enquiring into, and whether they are the means of happiness or of misery to mankind.

In the early ages of the world, according to the scripture chronology, there were no kings; the consequence of which was, there were no wars; it is the pride of kings which throw mankind into confusion. Holland without a king hath enjoyed more peace for this last century than any of the monarchial governments in Europe. Antiquity favors the same remark; for the quiet and rural lives of the first patriarchs hath a happy something in them, which vanishes away when we come to the history of Jewish royalty.

Government by kings was first introduced into the world by the Heathens, from whom the children of Israel copied the custom. It was the most prosperous invention the Devil ever set on foot for the promotion of idolatry. The Heathens paid divine honors to their deceased kings, and the Christian world hath improved on the plan by doing the same to their living ones. How impious is the title of sacred majesty applied to a worm, who in the midst of his splendor is crumbling into dust!

As the exalting one man so greatly above the rest cannot be justified on the equal rights of nature, so neither can it be defended on the authority of scripture; for the will of the Almighty, as declared by Gideon and the prophet Samuel, expressly disapproves of government by kings. All anti-monarchial parts of scripture have been very smoothly glossed over in monarchial governments, but they undoubtedly merit the attention of countries which have their governments yet to form. Render unto Caesar the things which are Caesar's is the scriptural doctrine of courts, yet it is no support of monarchial government, for the Jews at that time were without a king, and in a state of vassalage to the Romans.

Near three thousand years passed away from the Mosaic account of the creation, till the Jews under a national delusion requested a king. Till then their form of government (except in extraordinary cases, where the Almighty interposed) was a kind of republic administered by a judge and the elders of the tribes.

Kings they had none, and it was held sinful to acknowledge any being under that title but the Lord of Hosts. And when a man seriously reflects on the idolatrous homage which is paid to the persons of kings, he need not wonder that the Almighty, ever jealous of his honor, should disapprove of a form of government which so impiously invades the prerogative of heaven.

Monarchy is ranked in scripture as one of the sins of the Jews, for which a curse in reserve is denounced against them. The history of that transaction is worth attending to.

The children of Israel being oppressed by the Midianites, Gideon marched against them with a small army, and victory, through the divine interposition, decided in his favor. The Jews, elate with success, and attributing it to the generalship of Gideon, proposed making him a king, saying, Rule thou over us, thou and thy son and thy son's son. Here was temptation in its fullest extent; not a kingdom only, but an hereditary one, but Gideon in the piety of his soul replied, I will not rule over you, neither shall my son rule over you, THE LORD SHALL RULE OVER YOU. Words need not be more explicit; Gideon doth not decline the honor but denieth their right to give it; neither doth he compliment them with invented declarations of his thanks, but in the positive style of a prophet charges them with disaffection to their proper sovereign, the King of Heaven.

About one hundred and thirty years after this, they fell again into the same error. The hankering which the Jews had for the idolatrous customs of the Heathens, is something exceedingly unaccountable; but so it was, that laying hold of the misconduct of Samuel's two sons, who were entrusted with some secular concerns, they came in an abrupt and clamorous manner to Samuel, saying, Behold thou art old and thy sons walk not in thy ways, now make us a king to judge us like all the other nations. And here we cannot but observe that their motives were bad, viz., that they might be like unto other nations, i.e., the Heathen, whereas their true glory laid in being as much unlike them as possible. But the thing displeased Samuel when they said, Give us a king to judge us; and Samuel prayed unto the Lord, and the Lord said unto Samuel, Hearken unto the voice of the people in all that they say unto thee, for they have not rejected thee, but they have rejected me, THAT I SHOULD NOT REIGN OVER THEM.

According to all the works which have done since the day; wherewith they brought them up out of Egypt, even unto this day; wherewith they have forsaken me and served other Gods; so do they also unto thee. Now therefore hearken unto their voice, howbeit, protest solemnly unto them and show them the manner of the king that shall reign over them, i.e., not of any particular king, but the general manner of the kings of the earth, whom Israel was so eagerly copying after. And notwithstanding the great distance of time and difference of manners, the character is still in fashion. And Samuel told all the words of the Lord unto the people, that asked of him a king. And he said, This shall be the manner of the king that shall reign over you; he will take your sons and appoint them for himself for his chariots, and to be his horsemen, and some shall run before his chariots (this description agrees with the present mode of impressing men) and he will appoint him captains over thousands and captains over fifties, and will set them to ear his ground and to reap his harvest, and to make his instruments of war, and instruments of his chariots; and he will take your daughters to be confectionaries and to be cooks and to be bakers (this describes the expense and luxury as well as the oppression of kings) and he will take your fields and your olive yards, even the best of them, and give them to his servants; and he will take the tenth of your seed, and of your vineyards, and give them to his officers and to his servants (by which we see that bribery, corruption, and favoritism are the standing vices of kings) and he will take the tenth of your men servants, and your maid servants, and your goodliest young men and your asses, and put them to his work; and he will take the tenth of your sheep, and ye shall be his servants, and ye shall cry out in that day because of your king which ye shall have chosen, AND THE LORD WILL NOT HEAR YOU IN THAT DAY. This accounts for the continuation of monarchy; neither do the characters of the few good kings which have lived since, either sanctify the title, or blot out the sinfulness of the origin; the high encomium given of David takes no notice of him officially as a king, but only as a man after God's own heart. Nevertheless the People refused to obey the voice of Samuel, and they said, Nay, but we will have a king over us, that we may be like all the nations, and that our king may judge us, and go out before us and fight our battles. Samuel continued to reason with them, but to no purpose; he set before them their ingratitude, but all would not avail; and seeing them fully bent on their folly, he cried out, I will call unto the Lord, and he shall send thunder and rain (which then was a punishment, being the time of wheat harvest) that ye may perceive and see that your wickedness is great which ye have done in the sight of the Lord, IN ASKING YOU A KING. So Samuel called unto the Lord, and the Lord sent thunder and rain that day, and all the people greatly feared the Lord and Samuel and all the people said unto Samuel, Pray for thy servants unto the Lord thy God that we die not, for WE HAVE ADDED UNTO OUR SINS THIS EVIL, TO ASK A KING. These portions of scripture are direct and positive. They admit of no equivocal construction. That the Almighty hath here entered his protest against monarchial government is true, or the scripture is false. And a man hath good reason to believe that there is as much of kingcraft, as priestcraft in withholding the scripture from the public in Popish countries. For monarchy in every instance is the Popery of government.

To the evil of monarchy we have added that of hereditary succession; and as the first is a degradation and lessening of ourselves, so the second, claimed as a matter of right, is an insult and an imposition on posterity. For all men being originally equals, no one by birth could have a right to set up his own family in perpetual preference to all others for ever, and though himself might deserve some decent degree of honors of his contemporaries, yet his descendants might be far too unworthy to inherit them. One of the strongest natural proofs of the folly of hereditary right in kings, is, that nature disapproves it, otherwise she would not so frequently turn it into ridicule by giving mankind an ass for a lion.

Secondly, as no man at first could possess any other public honors than were bestowed upon him, so the givers of those honors could have no power to give away the right of posterity, and though they might say, "We choose you for our head," they could not, without manifest injustice to their children, say, "that your children and your children's children shall reign over ours for ever." Because such an unwise, unjust, unnatural compact might (perhaps) in the next succession put them under the government of a rogue or a fool. Most wise men, in their private sentiments, have ever treated hereditary right with contempt; yet it is one of those evils, which when once established is not easily removed; many submit from fear, others from superstition, and the more powerful part shares with the king the plunder of the rest.

This is supposing the present race of kings in the world to have had an honorable origin; whereas it is more than probable, that could we take off the dark covering of antiquities, and trace them to their first rise, that we should find the first of them nothing better than the principal ruffian of some restless gang, whose savage manners of preeminence in subtlety obtained him the title of chief among plunderers; and who by increasing in power, and extending his depredations, overawed the quiet and defenseless to purchase their safety by frequent contributions. Yet his electors could have no idea of giving hereditary right to his descendants, because such a perpetual exclusion of themselves was incompatible with the free and unrestrained principles they professed to live by. Wherefore, hereditary succession in the early ages of monarchy could not take place as a matter of claim, but as something casual or complemental; but as few or no records were extant in those days, and traditionary history stuffed with fables, it was very easy, after the lapse of a few generations, to trump up some superstitious tale, conveniently timed, Mahomet like, to cram hereditary right down the throats of the vulgar. Perhaps the disorders which threatened, or seemed to threaten on the decease of a leader and the choice of a new one (for elections among ruffians could not be very orderly) induced many at first to favor hereditary pretensions; by which means it happened, as it hath happened since, that what at first was submitted to as a convenience, was afterwards claimed as a right.

England, since the conquest, hath known some few good monarchs, but groaned beneath a much larger number of bad ones, yet no man in his senses can say that their claim under William the Conqueror is a very honorable one. A French bastard landing with an armed banditti, and establishing himself king of England against the consent of the natives, is in plain terms a very paltry rascally original. It certainly hath no divinity in it. However, it is needless to spend much time in exposing the folly of hereditary right, if there are any so weak as to believe it, let them promiscuously worship the ass and lion, and welcome. I shall neither copy their humility, nor disturb their devotion.

Yet I should be glad to ask how they suppose kings came at first? The question admits but of three answers, viz., either by lot, by election, or by usurpation. If the first king was taken by lot, it establishes a precedent for the next, which excludes hereditary succession. Saul was by lot, yet the succession was not hereditary, neither does it appear from that transaction there was any intention it ever should be. If the first king of any country was by election, that likewise establishes a precedent for the next; for to say, that the right of all future generations is taken away, by the act of the first electors, in their choice not only of a king, but of a family of kings for ever, hath no parallel in or out of scripture but the doctrine of original sin, which supposes the free will of all men lost in Adam; and from such comparison, and it will admit of no other, hereditary succession can derive no glory. For as in Adam all sinned, and as in the first electors all men obeyed; as in the one all mankind were subjected to Satan, and in the other to Sovereignty; as our innocence was lost in the first, and our authority in the last; and as both disable us from reassuming some former state and privilege, it unanswerably follows that original sin and hereditary succession are parallels. Dishonorable rank! Inglorious connection! Yet the most subtle sophist cannot produce a juster simile.

As to usurpation, no man will be so hardy as to defend it; and that William the Conqueror was an usurper is a fact not to be contradicted. The plain truth is, that the antiquity of English monarchy will not bear looking into.

But it is not so much the absurdity as the evil of hereditary succession which concerns mankind. Did it ensure a race of good and wise men it would have the seal of divine authority, but as it opens a door to the foolish, the wicked, and the improper, it hath in it the nature of oppression. Men who look upon themselves born to reign, and others to obey, soon grow insolent; selected from the rest of mankind their minds are early poisoned by importance; and the world they act in differs so materially from the world at large, that they have but little opportunity of knowing its true interests, and when they succeed to the government are frequently the most ignorant and unfit of any throughout the dominions.

Another evil which attends hereditary succession is, that the throne is subject to be possessed by a minor at any age; all which time the regency, acting under the cover of a king, have every opportunity and inducement to betray their trust. The same national misfortune happens, when a king, worn out with age and infirmity, enters the last stage of human weakness. In both these cases the public becomes a prey to every miscreant, who can tamper successfully with the follies either of age or infancy.

The most plausible plea, which hath ever been offered in favor of hereditary succession, is, that it preserves a nation from civil wars; and were this true, it would be weighty; whereas, it is the most barefaced falsity ever imposed upon mankind. The whole history of England disowns the fact. Thirty kings and two minors have reigned in that distracted kingdom since the conquest, in which time there have been (including the Revolution) no less than eight civil wars and nineteen rebellions. Wherefore instead of making for peace, it makes against it, and destroys the very foundation it seems to stand on.

The contest for monarchy and succession, between the houses of York and Lancaster, laid England in a scene of blood for many years. Twelve pitched battles, besides skirmishes and sieges, were fought between Henry and Edward. Twice was Henry prisoner to Edward, who in his turn was prisoner to Henry. And so uncertain is the fate of war and the temper of a nation, when nothing but personal matters are the ground of a quarrel, that Henry was taken in triumph from a prison to a palace, and Edward obliged to fly from a palace to a foreign land; yet, as sudden transitions of temper are seldom lasting, Henry in his turn was driven from the throne, and Edward recalled to succeed him. The parliament always following the strongest side.

This contest began in the reign of Henry the Sixth, and was not entirely extinguished till Henry the Seventh, in whom the families were united. Including a period of 67 years, viz., from 1422 to 1489.

In short, monarchy and succession have laid (not this or that kingdom only) but the world in blood and ashes. 'Tis a form of government which the word of God bears testimony against, and blood will attend it.

If we inquire into the business of a king, we shall find that (in some countries they have none) and after sauntering away their lives without pleasure to themselves or advantage to the nation, withdraw from the scene, and leave their successors to tread the same idle round. In absolute monarchies the whole weight of business, civil and military, lies on the king; the children of Israel in their request for a king, urged this plea "that he may judge us, and go out before us and fight our battles." But in countries where he is neither a judge nor a general, as in England, a man would be puzzled to know what is his business.

The nearer any government approaches to a republic, the less business there is for a king. It is somewhat difficult to find a proper name for the government of England. Sir William Meredith calls it a republic; but in its present state it is unworthy of the name, because the corrupt influence of the crown, by having all the places in its disposal, hath so effectually swallowed up the power, and eaten out the virtue of the house of commons (the republican part in the constitution) that the government of England is nearly as monarchical as that of France or Spain. Men fall out with names without understanding them. For it is the republican and not the monarchical part of the constitution of England which Englishmen glory in, viz., the liberty of choosing an house of commons from out of their own body—and it is easy to see that when the republican virtue fails, slavery ensues. Why is the constitution of England sickly, but because monarchy hath poisoned the republic, the crown hath engrossed the commons?

In England a king hath little more to do than to make war and give away places; which in plain terms, is to impoverish the nation and set it together by the ears. A pretty business indeed for a man to be allowed eight hundred thousand sterling a year for, and worshipped into the bargain! Of more worth is one honest man to society, and in the sight of God, than all the crowned ruffians that ever lived.

THOUGHTS ON THE
PRESENT STATE OF
AMERICAN AFFAIRS

In the following pages I offer nothing more than simple facts, plain arguments, and common sense; and have no other preliminaries to settle with the reader, than that he will divest himself of prejudice and prepossession, and suffer his reason and his feelings to determine for themselves; that he will put on, or rather that he will not put off the true character of a man, and generously enlarge his views beyond the present day.

Volumes have been written on the subject of the struggle between England and America. Men of all ranks have embarked in the controversy, from different motives, and with various designs; but all have been ineffectual, and the period of debate is closed. Arms, as the last resource, decide the contest; the appeal was the choice of the king, and the continent hath accepted the challenge.

It hath been reported of the late Mr. Pelham (who tho' an able minister was not without his faults) that on his being attacked in the house of commons, on the score, that his measures were only of a temporary kind, replied, "They will last my time." Should a thought so fatal and unmanly possess the colonies in the present contest, the name of ancestors will be remembered by future generations with detestation.

The sun never shined on a cause of greater worth. 'Tis not the affair of a city, a country, a province, or a kingdom, but of a continent—of at least one eighth part of the habitable globe. 'Tis not the concern of a day, a year, or an age; posterity are virtually involved in the contest, and will be more or less affected, even to the end of time, by the proceedings now. Now is the seed-time of continental union, faith and honor. The least fracture now will be like a name engraved with the point of a pin on the tender rind of a young oak; The wound will enlarge with the tree, and posterity read it in full grown characters.

By referring the matter from argument to arms, a new area for politics is struck; a new method of thinking hath arisen. All plans, proposals, &c. prior to the nineteenth of April, i.e., to the commencement of hostilities, are like the almanacs of the last year; which, though proper then, are superseded and useless now. Whatever was advanced by the advocates on either side of the question then, terminated in one and the same point, viz., a union with Great Britain; the only difference between the parties was the method of effecting it; the one proposing force, the other friendship; but it hath so far happened that the first hath failed, and the second hath withdrawn her influence.

As much hath been said of the advantages of reconciliation, which, like an agreeable dream, hath passed away and left us as we were, it is but right, that we should examine the contrary side of the argument, and inquire into some of the many material injuries which these colonies sustain, and always will sustain, by being connected with, and dependant on Great Britain. To examine that connection and dependance, on the principles of nature and common sense, to see what we have to trust to, if separated, and what we are to expect, if dependant.

I have heard it asserted by some, that as America hath flourished under her former connection with Great Britain, that the same connection is necessary towards her future happiness, and will always have the same effect. Nothing can be more fallacious than this kind of argument. We may as well assert, that because a child has thrived upon milk, that it is never to have meat; or that the first twenty years of our lives is to become a precedent for the next twenty. But even this is admitting more than is true, for I answer roundly, that America would have flourished as much, and probably much more, had no European power had any thing to do with her. The commerce by which she hath enriched herself are the necessaries of life, and will always have a market while eating is the custom of Europe.

But she has protected us, say some. That she hath engrossed us is true, and defended the continent at our expense as well as her own is admitted, and she would have defended Turkey from the same motive, viz., the sake of trade and dominion.

Alas! We have been long led away by ancient prejudices and made large sacrifices to superstition. We have boasted the protection of Great Britain, without considering, that her motive was interest not attachment; that she did not protect us from our enemies on our account, but from her enemies on her own account, from those who had no quarrel with us on any other account, and who will always be our enemies on the same account. Let Britain wave her pretensions to the continent, or the continent throw off the dependance, and we should be at peace with France and Spain were they at war with Britain. The miseries of Hanover last war, ought to warn us against connections.

It hath lately been asserted in parliament, that the colonies have no relation to each other but through the parent country, i.e., that Pennsylvania and the Jerseys, and so on for the rest, are sister colonies by the way of England; this is certainly a very roundabout way of proving relationship, but it is the nearest and only true way of proving enemyship, if I may so call it. France and Spain never were, nor perhaps ever will be our enemies as Americans, but as our being the subjects of Great Britain.

But Britain is the parent country, say some. Then the more shame upon her conduct. Even brutes do not devour their young; nor savages make war upon their families; wherefore the assertion, if true, turns to her reproach; but it happens not to be true, or only partly so, and the phrase parent or mother country hath been jesuitically adopted by the king and his parasites, with a low papistical design of gaining an unfair bias on the credulous weakness of our minds. Europe, and not England, is the parent country of America. This new world hath been the asylum for the persecuted lovers of civil and religious liberty from every Part of Europe. Hither have they fled, not from the tender embraces of the mother, but from the cruelty of the monster; and it is so far true of England, that the same tyranny which drove the first emigrants from home pursues their descendants still.

In this extensive quarter of the globe, we forget the narrow limits of three hundred and sixty miles (the extent of England) and carry our friendship on a larger scale; we claim brotherhood with every European Christian, and triumph in the generosity of the sentiment.

It is pleasant to observe by what regular gradations we surmount the force of local prejudice, as we enlarge our acquaintance with the world. A man born in any town in England divided into parishes, will naturally associate most with his fellow parishioners (because their interests in many cases will be common) and distinguish him by the name of neighbor; if he meet him but a few miles from home, he drops the narrow idea of a street, and salutes him by the name of townsman; if he travels out of the county, and meet him in any other, he forgets the minor divisions of street and town, and calls him countryman; i.e., countyman; but if in their foreign excursions they should associate in France or any other part of Europe, their local remembrance would be enlarged into that of Englishmen. And by a just parity of reasoning, all Europeans meeting in America, or any other quarter of the globe, are countrymen; for England, Holland, Germany, or Sweden, when compared with the whole, stand in the same places on the larger scale, which the divisions of street, town, and county do on the smaller ones; distinctions too limited for continental minds. Not one third of the inhabitants, even of this province, are of English descent. Wherefore, I reprobate the phrase of parent or mother country applied to England only, as being false, selfish, narrow and ungenerous.

But admitting that we were all of English descent, what does it amount to? Nothing. Britain, being now an open enemy, extinguishes every other name and title: And to say that reconciliation is our duty, is truly farcical. The first king of England, of the present line (William the Conqueror) was a Frenchman, and half the peers of England are descendants from the same country; wherefore by the same method of reasoning, England ought to be governed by France.

Much hath been said of the united strength of Britain and the colonies, that in conjunction they might bid defiance to the world. But this is mere presumption; the fate of war is uncertain, neither do the expressions mean any thing; for this continent would never suffer itself to be drained of inhabitants to support the British arms in either Asia, Africa, or Europe.

Besides, what have we to do with setting the world at defiance? Our plan is commerce, and that, well attended to, will secure us the peace and friendship of all Europe; because it is the interest of all Europe to have America a free port. Her trade will always be a protection, and her barrenness of gold and silver secure her from invaders.

I challenge the warmest advocate for reconciliation, to show, a single advantage that this continent can reap, by being connected with Great Britain. I repeat the challenge, not a single advantage is derived. Our corn will fetch its price in any market in Europe, and our imported goods must be paid for buy them where we will.

But the injuries and disadvantages we sustain by that connection, are without number; and our duty to mankind at large, as well as to ourselves, instruct us to renounce the alliance: Because, any submission to, or dependance on Great Britain, tends directly to involve this continent in European wars and quarrels; and sets us at variance with nations, who would otherwise seek our friendship, and against whom, we have neither anger nor complaint. As Europe is our market for trade, we ought to form no partial connection with any part of it. It is the true interest of America to steer clear of European contentions, which she never can do, while by her dependance on Britain, she is made the make-weight in the scale of British politics.

Europe is too thickly planted with kingdoms to be long at peace, and whenever a war breaks out between England and any foreign power, the trade of America goes to ruin, because of her connection with Britain. The next war may not turn out like the last, and should it not, the advocates for reconciliation now will be wishing for separation then, because, neutrality in that case, would be a safer convoy than a man of war. Every thing that is right or natural pleads for separation. The blood of the slain, the weeping voice of nature cries, 'tis time to part. Even the distance at which the Almighty hath placed England and America, is a strong and natural proof, that the authority of the one, over the other, was never the design of Heaven. The time likewise at which

the continent was discovered, adds weight to the argument, and
the manner in which it was peopled increases the force of it. The
reformation was preceded by the discovery of America, as if the
Almighty graciously meant to open a sanctuary to the persecuted
in future years, when home should afford neither friendship nor
safety.

The authority of Great Britain over this continent, is a form
of government, which sooner or later must have an end: And a serious mind can draw no true pleasure by looking forward, under
the painful and positive conviction, that what he calls "the present constitution" is merely temporary. As parents, we can have
no joy, knowing that this government is not sufficiently lasting
to ensure any thing which we may bequeath to posterity: And by
a plain method of argument, as we are running the next generation into debt, we ought to do the work of it, otherwise we use
them meanly and pitifully. In order to discover the line of our
duty rightly, we should take our children in our hand, and fix our
station a few years farther into life; that eminence will present a
prospect, which a few present fears and prejudices conceal from
our sight.

Though I would carefully avoid giving unnecessary offence,
yet I am inclined to believe, that all those who espouse the doctrine of reconciliation, may be included within the following de-
scriptions: Interested men, who are not to be trusted; weak men
who cannot see; prejudiced men, who will not see; and a certain
set of moderate men, who think better of the European world
than it deserves; and this last class, by an ill-judged deliberation,
will be the cause of more calamities to this continent than all the
other three.

It is the good fortune of many to live distant from the scene of
sorrow; the evil is not sufficiently brought to their doors to make

them feel the precariousness with which all American property is possessed. But let our imaginations transport us for a few moments to Boston, that seat of wretchedness will teach us wisdom, and instruct us for ever to renounce a power in whom we can have no trust. The inhabitants of that unfortunate city, who but a few months ago were in ease and affluence, have now no other alternative than to stay and starve, or turn out to beg. Endangered by the fire of their friends if they continue within the city, and plundered by the soldiery if they leave it. In their present condition they are prisoners without the hope of redemption, and in a general attack for their relief, they would be exposed to the fury of both armies.

Men of passive tempers look somewhat lightly over the offenses of Britain, and, still hoping for the best, are apt to call out, Come, we shall be friends again for all this. But examine the passions and feelings of mankind. Bring the doctrine of reconciliation to the touchstone of nature, and then tell me, whether you can hereafter love, honor, and faithfully serve the power that hath carried fire and sword into your land? If you cannot do all these, then are you only deceiving yourselves, and by your delay bringing ruin upon posterity. Your future connection with Britain, whom you can neither love nor honor, will be forced and unnatural, and being formed only on the plan of present convenience, will in a little time fall into a relapse more wretched than the first. But if you say, you can still pass the violations over, then I ask, Hath your house been burnt? Hath you property been destroyed before your face? Are your wife and children destitute of a bed to lie on, or bread to live on? Have you lost a parent or a child by their hands, and yourself the ruined and wretched survivor? If you have not, then are you not a judge of those who have. But if you have, and can still shake hands with the murderers, then are you unworthy of the name of husband, father, friend, or lover, and whatever may be your rank or title in life, you have the heart of a coward, and the spirit of a sycophant.

This is not inflaming or exaggerating matters, but trying them by those feelings and affections which nature justifies, and without which, we should be incapable of discharging the social duties of life, or enjoying the felicities of it. I mean not to exhibit horror for the purpose of provoking revenge, but to awaken us from fatal and unmanly slumbers, that we may pursue determinately some fixed object. It is not in the power of Britain or of Europe to conquer America, if she do not conquer herself by delay and timidity. The present winter is worth an age if rightly employed, but if lost or neglected, the whole continent will partake of the misfortune; and there is no punishment which that man will not deserve, be he who, or what, or where he will, that may be the means of sacrificing a season so precious and useful.

It is repugnant to reason, to the universal order of things, to all examples from the former ages, to suppose, that this continent can longer remain subject to any external power. The most sanguine in Britain does not think so. The utmost stretch of human wisdom cannot, at this time, compass a plan short of separation, which can promise the continent even a year's security. Reconciliation is now a fallacious dream. Nature hath deserted the connection, and Art cannot supply her place. For, as Milton wisely expresses, "never can true reconcilement grow where wounds of deadly hate have pierced so deep."

Every quiet method for peace hath been ineffectual. Our prayers have been rejected with disdain; and only tended to convince us, that nothing flatters vanity, or confirms obstinacy in kings more than repeated petitioning—and nothing hath contributed more than that very measure to make the kings of Europe absolute: Witness Denmark and Sweden. Wherefore since nothing but blows will do, for God's sake, let us come to a final separation, and not leave the next generation to be cutting throats, under the violated unmeaning names of parent and child.

To say, they will never attempt it again is idle and visionary, we thought so at the repeal of the stamp act, yet a year or two undeceived us; as well may we suppose that nations, which have been once defeated, will never renew the quarrel.

As to government matters, it is not in the powers of Britain to do this continent justice: The business of it will soon be too weighty, and intricate, to be managed with any tolerable degree of convenience, by a power so distant from us, and so very ignorant of us; for if they cannot conquer us, they cannot govern us. To be always running three or four thousand miles with a tale or a petition, waiting four or five months for an answer, which when obtained requires five or six more to explain it in, will in a few years be looked upon as folly and childishness—there was a time when it was proper, and there is a proper time for it to cease.

Small islands not capable of protecting themselves, are the proper objects for kingdoms to take under their care; but there is something very absurd, in supposing a continent to be perpetually governed by an island. In no instance hath nature made the satellite larger than its primary planet, and as England and America, with respect to each other, reverses the common order of nature, it is evident they belong to different systems: England to Europe—America to itself.

I am not induced by motives of pride, party, or resentment to espouse the doctrine of separation and independance; I am clearly, positively, and conscientiously persuaded that it is the true interest of this continent to be so; that every thing short of that is mere patchwork, that it can afford no lasting felicity, —that it is leaving the sword to our children, and shrinking back at a time, when, a little more, a little farther, would have rendered this continent the glory of the earth.

As Britain hath not manifested the least inclination towards a compromise, we may be assured that no terms can be obtained worthy the acceptance of the continent, or any ways equal to the expense of blood and treasure we have been already put to.

The object contended for, ought always to bear some just proportion to the expense. The removal of the North, or the whole detestable junto, is a matter unworthy the millions we have expended. A temporary stoppage of trade, was an inconvenience, which would have sufficiently balanced the repeal of all the acts complained of, had such repeals been obtained; but if the whole continent must take up arms, if every man must be a soldier, it is scarcely worth our while to fight against a contemptible ministry only. Dearly, dearly, do we pay for the repeal of the acts, if that is all we fight for; for in a just estimation, it is as great a folly to pay a Bunker Hill price for law, as for land. As I have always considered the independancy of this continent, as an event, which sooner or later must arrive, so from the late rapid progress of the continent to maturity, the event could not be far off. Wherefore, on the breaking out of hostilities, it was not worth the while to have disputed a matter, which time would have finally redressed, unless we meant to be in earnest; otherwise, it is like wasting an estate on a suit at law, to regulate the trespasses of a tenant, whose lease is just expiring. No man was a warmer wisher for reconciliation than myself, before the fatal nineteenth of April, 1775 (Massacre at Lexington), but the moment the event of that day was made known, I rejected the hardened, sullen tempered Pharaoh of England for ever; and disdain the wretch, that with the pretended title of Father of His People, can unfeelingly hear of their slaughter, and composedly sleep with their blood upon his soul.

But admitting that matters were now made up, what would be the event? I answer, the ruin of the continent. And that for several reasons:

First. The powers of governing still remaining in the hands of the king, he will have a negative over the whole legislation of this continent. And as he hath shown himself such an inveterate enemy to liberty, and discovered such a thirst for arbitrary power, is he, or is he not, a proper man to say to these colonies, "You shall make no laws but what I please?" And is there any inhabitant in America so ignorant, as not to know, that according to what is called the present constitution, that this continent can make no laws but what the king gives leave to? And is there any man so unwise, as not to see, that (considering what has happened) he will suffer no Law to be made here, but such as suit his purpose? We may be as effectually enslaved by the want of laws in America, as by submitting to laws made for us in England. After matters are made up (as it is called) can there be any doubt but the whole power of the crown will be exerted, to keep this continent as low and humble as possible? Instead of going forward we shall go backward, or be perpetually quarrelling or ridiculously petitioning. We are already greater than the king wishes us to be, and will he not hereafter endeavor to make us less? To bring the matter to one point. Is the power who is jealous of our prosperity, a proper power to govern us? Whoever says No to this question is an independant, for independancy means no more, than, whether we shall make our own laws, or whether the king, the greatest enemy this continent hath, or can have, shall tell us, "there shall be no laws but such as I like."

But the king you will say has a negative in England; the people there can make no laws without his consent. In point of right and good order, there is something very ridiculous, that a youth of twenty-one (which hath often happened) shall say to several millions of people, older and wiser than himself, I forbid this or that act of yours to be law. But in this place I decline this sort of reply, though I will never cease to expose the absurdity of it, and only answer, that England being the king's residence, and America not so, make quite another case. The king's negative here is ten times more dangerous and fatal than it can be in England, for there he will scarcely refuse his consent to a bill for putting England into as strong a state of defence as possible, and in America he would never suffer such a bill to be passed.

America is only a secondary object in the system of British politics—England consults the good of this country, no farther than it answers her own purpose. Wherefore, her own interest leads her to suppress the growth of ours in every case which doth not promote her advantage, or in the least interferes with it. A pretty state we should soon be in under such a second-hand government, considering what has happened! Men do not change from enemies to friends by the alteration of a name; and in order to show that reconciliation now is a dangerous doctrine, I affirm, that it would be policy in the kingdom at this time, to repeal the acts for the sake of reinstating himself in the government of the provinces; in order, that he may accomplish by craft and subtlety, in the long run, what he cannot do by force and violence in the short one. Reconciliation and ruin are nearly related.

Secondly. That as even the best terms, which we can expect to obtain, can amount to no more than a temporary expedient, or a kind of government by guardianship, which can last no longer than till the colonies come of age, so the general face and state of things, in the interim, will be unsettled and unpromising. Emigrants of property will not choose to come to a country whose form of government hangs but by a thread, and who is every day tottering on the brink of commotion and disturbance; and numbers of the present inhabitants would lay hold of the interval, to dispose of their effects, and quit the continent.

But the most powerful of all arguments, is, that nothing but independance, i.e., a continental form of government, can keep the peace of the continent and preserve it inviolate from civil wars. I dread the event of a reconciliation with Britain now, as it is more than probable, that it will be followed by a revolt somewhere or other, the consequences of which may be far more fatal than all the malice of Britain.

Thousands are already ruined by British barbarity; (thousands more will probably suffer the same fate.) Those men have other feelings than us who have nothing suffered. All they now possess is liberty, what they before enjoyed is sacrificed to its service, and having nothing more to lose, they disdain submission. Besides, the general temper of the colonies, towards a British government, will be like that of a youth, who is nearly out of his time, they will care very little about her. And a government which cannot preserve the peace, is no government at all, and in that case we pay our money for nothing; and pray what is it that Britain can do, whose power will be wholly on paper, should a civil tumult break out the very day after reconciliation? I have heard some men say, many of whom I believe spoke without thinking, that they dreaded independance, fearing that it would produce civil wars. It is but seldom that our first thoughts are truly correct, and that is the case here; for there are ten times more to dread from a patched up connection than from independance. I make the sufferers case my own, and I protest, that were I driven from house and home, my property destroyed, and my circumstances ruined, that as man, sensible of injuries, I could never relish the doctrine of reconciliation, or consider myself bound thereby.

The colonies have manifested such a spirit of good order and obedience to continental government, as is sufficient to make every reasonable person easy and happy on that head. No man can assign the least pretence for his fears, on any other grounds, that such as are truly childish and ridiculous, viz., that one colony will be striving for superiority over another.

Where there are no distinctions there can be no superiority, perfect equality affords no temptation. The republics of Europe are all (and we may say always) in peace. Holland and Switzerland are without wars, foreign or domestic; monarchical governments, it is true, are never long at rest: the crown itself is a temptation to enterprising ruffians at home; and that degree of pride and insolence ever attendant on regal authority swells into a rupture with foreign powers, in instances where a republican government, by being formed on more natural principles, would negotiate the mistake.

If there is any true cause of fear respecting independance it is because no plan is yet laid down. Men do not see their way out; wherefore, as an opening into that business I offer the following hints; at the same time modestly affirming, that I have no other opinion of them myself, than that they may be the means of giving rise to something better. Could the straggling thoughts of individuals be collected, they would frequently form materials for wise and able men to improve to useful matter.

Let the assemblies be annual, with a President only. The representation more equal. Their business wholly domestic, and subject to the authority of a Continental Congress.

Let each colony be divided into six, eight, or ten, convenient districts, each district to send a proper number of delegates to Congress, so that each colony send at least thirty. The whole number in Congress will be at least three hundred ninety. Each Congress to sit . . . and to choose a president by the following method. When the delegates are met, let a colony be taken from the whole thirteen colonies by lot, after which let the whole Congress choose (by ballot) a president from out of the delegates of that province. In the next Congress, let a colony be taken by lot from twelve only, omitting that colony from which the president was taken in the former Congress, and so proceeding on till the whole thirteen shall have had their proper rotation. And in order that nothing may pass into a law but what is satisfactorily just, not less than three fifths of the Congress to be called a majority. He that will promote discord, under a government so equally formed as this, would join Lucifer in his revolt.

But as there is a peculiar delicacy, from whom, or in what manner, this business must first arise, and as it seems most agreeable and consistent, that it should come from some intermediate body between the governed and the governors, that is, between the Congress and the people, let a Continental Conference be held, in the following manner, and for the following purpose:

A committee of twenty-six members of Congress, viz., two for each colony. Two members for each house of assembly, or provincial convention; and five representatives of the people at large, to be chosen in the capital city or town of each province, for, and in behalf of the whole province, by as many qualified voters as shall think proper to attend from all parts of the province for that purpose; or, if more convenient, the representatives may be chosen in two or three of the most populous parts thereof. In this conference, thus assembled, will be united, the two grand principles of business, knowledge and power. The members of Congress, Assemblies, or Conventions, by having had experience in national concerns, will be able and useful counsellors, and the whole, being empowered by the people will have a truly legal authority.

The conferring members being met, let their business be to frame a Continental Charter, or Charter of the United Colonies; (answering to what is called the Magna Carta of England) fixing .

the number and manner of choosing members of Congress, members of Assembly, with their date of sitting, and drawing the line of business and jurisdiction between them: always remembering, that our strength is continental, not provincial: Securing freedom and property to all men, and above all things the free exercise of religion, according to the dictates of conscience; with such other matter as is necessary for a charter to contain. Immediately after which, the said conference to dissolve, and the bodies which shall be chosen conformable to the said charter, to be the legislators and governors of this continent for the time being: Whose peace and happiness, may God preserve, Amen.

Should any body of men be hereafter delegated for this or some similar purpose, I offer them the following extracts from that wise observer on governments Dragonetti. "The science" says he, "of the politician consists in fixing the true point of happiness and freedom. Those men would deserve the gratitude of ages, who should discover a mode of government that contained the greatest sum of individual happiness, with the least national expense."—Dragonetti on Virtue and Rewards.

But where, says some, is the King of America? I'll tell you Friend, he reigns above, and doth not make havoc of mankind like the Royal Brute of Britain. Yet that we may not appear to be defective even in earthly honors, let a day be solemnly set apart for proclaiming the charter; let it be brought forth placed on the divine law, the word of God; let a crown be placed thereon, by which the world may know, that so far as we approve of monarchy, that in America the law is king. For as in absolute governments the king is law, so in free countries the law ought to be king; and there ought to be no other. But lest any ill use should afterwards arise, let the crown at the conclusion of the ceremony be demolished, and scattered among the people whose right it is.

A government of our own is our natural right: And when a man seriously reflects on the precariousness of human affairs, he will become convinced, that it is infinitely wiser and safer, to form a constitution of our own in a cool deliberate manner, while we have it in our power, than to trust such an interesting event to time and chance. If we omit it now, some Massenello* may hereafter arise, who laying hold of popular disquietudes, may collect together the desperate and the discontented, and by assuming to themselves the powers of government, may sweep away the liberties of the continent like a deluge. Should the government of America return again into the hands of Britain, the tottering situation of things, will be a temptation for some desperate adventurer to try his fortune; and in such a case, what relief can Britain give? Ere she could hear the news, the fatal business might be done, and ourselves suffering like the wretched Britons under the oppression of the Conqueror. Ye that oppose independance now, ye know not what ye do; ye are opening a door to eternal tyranny, by keeping vacant the seat of government.

There are thousands and tens of thousands; who would think it glorious to expel from the continent, that barbarous and hellish power, which hath stirred up the Indians and Negroes to destroy us; the cruelty hath a double guilt, it is dealing brutally by us, and treacherously by them. To talk of friendship with those in whom our reason forbids us to have faith, and our affections, (wounded through a thousand pores) instruct us to detest, is madness and folly. Every day wears out the little remains of kindred between us and them, and can there be any reason to hope, that as the

* Thomas Anello, otherwise Massenello, a fisherman of Naples, who after spiriting up his countrymen in the public marketplace, against the oppression of the Spaniards, to whom the place was then subject, prompted them to revolt, and in the space of a day became king.

relationship expires, the affection will increase, or that we shall agree better, when we have ten times more and greater concerns to quarrel over than ever?

Ye that tell us of harmony and reconciliation, can ye restore to us the time that is past? Can ye give to prostitution its former innocence? Neither can ye reconcile Britain and America. The last cord now is broken, the people of England are presenting addresses against us. There are injuries which nature cannot forgive; she would cease to be nature if she did. As well can the lover forgive the ravisher of his mistress, as the continent forgive the murders of Britain. The Almighty hath implanted in us these inextinguishable feelings for good and wise purposes. They are the guardians of his image in our hearts. They distinguish us from the herd of common animals. The social compact would dissolve, and justice be extirpated the earth, or have only a casual existence were we callous to the touches of affection. The robber and the murderer, would often escape unpunished, did not the injuries which our tempers sustain, provoke us into justice.

O ye that love mankind! Ye that dare oppose, not only the tyranny, but the tyrant, stand forth! Every spot of the old world is overrun with oppression. Freedom hath been hunted round the globe. Asia, and Africa, have long expelled her. Europe regards her like a stranger, and England hath given her warning to depart. O! receive the fugitive, and prepare in time an asylum for mankind.

OF THE PRESENT
ABILITY OF AMERICA,
WITH SOME
MISCELLANEOUS
REFLECTIONS

I have never met with a man, either in England or America, who hath not confessed his opinion, that a separation between the countries, would take place one time or other. And there is no instance in which we have shown less judgment, than in endeavoring to describe, what we call, the ripeness or fitness of the Continent for independance.

As all men allow the measure, and vary only in their opinion of the time, let us, in order to remove mistakes, take a general survey of things and endeavor if possible, to find out the very time. But we need not go far, the inquiry ceases at once, for the time hath found us. The general concurrence, the glorious union of all things prove the fact.

It is not in numbers but in unity, that our great strength lies;

yet our present numbers are sufficient to repel the force of all the world. The Continent hath, at this time, the largest body of armed and disciplined men of any power under Heaven; and is just arrived at that pitch of strength, in which no single colony is able to support itself, and the whole, who united can accomplish the matter, and either more, or, less than this, might be fatal in its effects. Our land force is already sufficient, and as to naval affairs, we cannot be insensible, that Britain would never suffer an American man of war to be built while the continent remained in her hands. Wherefore we should be no forwarder an hundred years hence in that branch, than we are now; but the truth is, we should be less so, because the timber of the country is every day diminishing, and that which will remain at last, will be far off and difficult to procure.

Were the continent crowded with inhabitants, her sufferings under the present circumstances would be intolerable. The more seaport towns we had, the more should we have both to defend and to lose. Our present numbers are so happily proportioned to our wants, that no man need be idle. The diminution of trade affords an army, and the necessities of an army create a new trade.

Debts we have none; and whatever we may contract on this account will serve as a glorious memento of our virtue. Can we but leave posterity with a settled form of government, an independant constitution of its own, the purchase at any price will be cheap. But to expend millions for the sake of getting a few vile acts repealed, and routing the present ministry only, is unworthy the charge, and is using posterity with the utmost cruelty; because it is leaving them the great work to do, and a debt upon their backs, from which they derive no advantage. Such a thought is unworthy of a man of honor, and is the true characteristic of a narrow heart and a peddling politician.

The debt we may contract doth not deserve our regard if the

work be but accomplished. No nation ought to be without a debt. A national debt is a national bond; and when it bears no interest, is in no case a grievance. Britain is oppressed with a debt of upwards of one hundred and forty millions sterling, for which she pays upwards of four millions interest. And as a compensation for her debt, she has a large navy; America is without a debt, and without a navy; yet for the twentieth part of the English national debt, could have a navy as large again. The navy of England is not worth, at this time, more than three millions and a half sterling.

The first and second editions of this pamphlet were published without the following calculations, which are now given as a proof that the above estimation of the navy is a just one. (See Entick's naval history, intro. page 56.)

The charge of building a ship of each rate, and furnishing her with masts, yards, sails and rigging, together with a proportion of eight months boatswain's and carpenter's sea-stores, as calculated by Mr. Burchett, Secretary to the navy, is as follows:

For a ship of 100 guns	£35,553
90	£29,886
80	£23,638
70	£17,785
60	£14,197
50	£10,606
40	£7,558
30	£5,846
20	£3,710

And from hence it is easy to sum up the value, or cost rather, of the whole British navy, which in the year 1757, when it was as its greatest glory consisted of the following ships and guns:

Ships	Guns	Cost of one	Cost of all
6	100	£35,533	£213,318
12	90	£29,886	£358,632
12	80	£23,638	£283,656
43	70	£17,785	£764,755
35	60	£14,197	£496,895
40	50	£10,606	£424,240
45	40	£7,758	£340,110
58	20	£3,710	£215,180
85 Sloops, bombs, and fireships, one another		£2,000	£170,000

Cost	£3,266,786
Remains for guns	£233,214
Total	£3,500,000

No country on the globe is so happily situated, so internally capable of raising a fleet as America. Tar, timber, iron, and cordage are her natural produce. We need go abroad for nothing. Whereas the Dutch, who make large profits by hiring out their ships of war to the Spaniards and Portuguese, are obliged to import most of the materials they use. We ought to view the building a fleet as an article of commerce, it being the natural manufactory of this country. It is the best money we can lay out. A navy when finished is worth more than it cost. And is that nice point in national policy, in which commerce and protection are united. Let us build; if we want them not, we can sell; and by the means replace our paper currency with ready gold and silver.

In point of manning a fleet, people in general run into great errors; it is not necessary that one-fourth part should be sailors. The privateer Terrible, Captain Death, stood the hottest engagement of any ship last war, yet had not twenty sailors on board, though her complement of men was upwards of two hundred. A few able and social sailors will soon instruct a sufficient number of active landsmen in the common work of a ship. Wherefore, we never can be more capable to begin on maritime matters than now, while our timber is standing, our fisheries blocked up, and our sailors and shipwrights out of employ. Men of war of seventy and eighty guns were built forty years ago in New England, and why not the same now? Ship building is America's greatest pride, and in which, she will in time excel the whole world. The great empires of the east are mostly inland, and consequently excluded from the possibility of rivalling her. Africa is in a state of barbarism; and no power in Europe hath either such an extent or coast, or such an internal supply of materials. Where nature hath given the one, she has withheld the other; to America only hath she been liberal of both. The vast empire of Russia is almost shut out from the sea; wherefore, her boundless forests, her tar, iron, and cordage are only articles of commerce.

In point of safety, ought we to be without a fleet? We are not the little people now, which we were sixty years ago; at that time we might have trusted our property in the streets, or fields rather; and slept securely without locks or bolts to our doors or windows. The case now is altered, and our methods of defence ought to improve with our increase of property. A common pirate, twelve months ago, might have come up the Delaware, and laid the city of Philadelphia under instant contribution, for what sum he pleased; and the same might have happened to other places. Nay, any daring fellow, in a brig of fourteen or sixteen guns, might have robbed the whole Continent, and carried off half a million of money. These are circumstances which demand our attention, and point out the necessity of naval protection.

Some, perhaps, will say, that after we have made it up with Britain, she will protect us. Can we be so unwise as to mean, that she shall keep a navy in our harbors for that purpose? Common sense will tell us, that the power which hath endeavored to subdue us, is of all others the most improper to defend us. Conquest may be effected under the pretence of friendship; and ourselves, after a long and brave resistance, be at last cheated into slavery. And if her ships are not to be admitted into our harbors, I would ask, how is she to protect us? A navy three or four thousand miles off can be of little use, and on sudden emergencies, none at all. Wherefore, if we must hereafter protect ourselves, why not do it for ourselves? Why do it for another?

The English list of ships of war is long and formidable, but not a tenth part of them are at any one time fit for service, numbers of them not in being; yet their names are pompously continued in the list, if only a plank be left of the ship: and not a fifth part, of such as are fit for service, can be spared on any one station at one time. The East and West Indies, Mediterranean, Africa, and other parts over which Britain extends her claim, make large demands upon her navy. From a mixture of prejudice and inattention, we have contracted a false notion respecting the navy of England, and have talked as if we should have the whole of it to encounter at once, and for that reason, supposed that we must have one as large; which not being instantly practicable, have been made use of by a set of disguised Tories to discourage our beginning thereon. Nothing can be farther from truth than this; for if America had only a twentieth part of the naval force of Britain, she would be by far an over match for her; because, as we neither have, nor claim any foreign dominion, our whole force would be employed on our own coast, where we should, in the long run, have two to one the advantage of those who had three or four thousand miles to sail over, before they could attack us, and the same distance to return in order to refit and recruit. And although Britain by her fleet, hath a check over our trade to Europe, we have as large a one over her trade to the West Indies, which, by laying in the neighborhood of the Continent, is entirely at its mercy.

Some method might be fallen on to keep up a naval force in time of peace, if we should not judge it necessary to support a constant navy. If premiums were to be given to merchants, to build and employ in their service, ships mounted with twenty, thirty, forty, or fifty guns, (the premiums to be in proportion to the loss of bulk to the merchants) fifty or sixty of those ships, with a few guard ships on constant duty, would keep up a sufficient navy, and that without burdening ourselves with the evil so loudly complained of in England, of suffering their fleet, in time of peace to lie rotting in the docks. To unite the sinews of commerce and defence is sound policy; for when our strength and our riches play into each other's hand, we need fear no external enemy.

In almost every article of defence we abound. Hemp flourishes even to rankness, so that we need not want cordage. Our iron is superior to that of other countries. Our small arms equal to any in the world. Cannon we can cast at pleasure. Saltpetre and gunpowder we are every day producing. Our knowledge is hourly improving. Resolution is our inherent character, and courage hath never yet forsaken us. Wherefore, what is it that we want? Why is it that we hesitate? From Britain we can expect nothing but ruin. If she is once admitted to the government of America again, this Continent will not be worth living in. Jealousies will be always arising; insurrections will be constantly happening; and who will go forth to quell them? Who will venture his life to reduce his own countrymen to a foreign obedience? The difference between Pennsylvania and Connecticut, respecting some unlocated lands, shows the insignificance of a British government, and fully proves, that nothing but Continental authority can regulate Continental matters.

Another reason why the present time is preferable to all others, is, that the fewer our numbers are, the more land there is yet unoccupied, which instead of being lavished by the king on his worthless dependants, may be hereafter applied, not only to the discharge of the present debt, but to the constant support of government. No nation under heaven hath such an advantage as this.

The infant state of the Colonies, as it is called, so far from being against, is an argument in favor of independance. We are sufficiently numerous, and were we more so, we might be less united. It is a matter worthy of observation, that the more a country is peopled, the smaller their armies are. In military numbers, the ancients far exceeded the moderns: and the reason is evident, for trade being the consequence of population, men become too much absorbed thereby to attend to anything else. Commerce diminishes the spirit, both of patriotism and military defence. And history sufficiently informs us, that the bravest achievements were always accomplished in the non-age of a nation. With the increase of commerce, England hath lost its spirit. The city of London, notwithstanding its numbers, submits to continued insults with the patience of a coward. The more men have to lose, the less willing are they to venture. The rich are in general slaves to fear, and submit to courtly power with the trembling duplicity of a spaniel.

Youth is the seed-time of good habits, as well in nations as in individuals. It might be difficult, if not impossible, to form the Continent into one government half a century hence. The vast variety of interests, occasioned by an increase of trade and population, would create confusion. Colony would be against colony. Each being able might scorn each other's assistance: and while the proud and foolish gloried in their little distinctions, the wise would lament that the union had not been formed before. Wherefore, the present time is the true time for establishing it. The intimacy which is contracted in infancy, and the friendship which is formed in misfortune, are, of all others, the most lasting and unalterable. Our present union is marked with both these characters: we are young, and we have been distressed; but our concord hath withstood our troubles, and fixes a memorable area for posterity to glory in.

The present time, likewise, is that peculiar time, which never happens to a nation but once, viz., the time of forming itself into a government. Most nations have let slip the opportunity, and by that means have been compelled to receive laws from their conquerors, instead of making laws for themselves. First, they had a king, and then a form of government; whereas, the articles or charter of government, should be formed first, and men delegated to execute them afterwards: but from the errors of other nations, let us learn wisdom, and lay hold of the present opportunity—to begin government at the right end.

When William the Conqueror subdued England he gave them law at the point of the sword; and until we consent that the seat of government in America, be legally and authoritatively occupied, we shall be in danger of having it filled by some fortunate ruffian, who may treat us in the same manner, and then, where will be our freedom? where our property?

As to religion, I hold it to be the indispensable duty of all government, to protect all conscientious professors thereof, and I know of no other business which government hath to do therewith. Let a man throw aside that narrowness of soul, that selfishness of principle, which the niggards of all professions are so unwilling to part with, and he will be at once delivered of his fears on that head. Suspicion is the companion of mean souls, and the bane of all good society. For myself I fully and conscientiously believe, that it is the will of the Almighty, that there should be diversity of religious opinions among us: It affords a larger field for our Christian kindness. Were we all of one way of thinking, our religious dispositions would want matter for probation; and on this liberal principle, I look on the various denominations among us, to be like children of the same family, differing only, in what is called their Christian names.

Earlier in this work, I threw out a few thoughts on the propriety of a Continental Charter, (for I only presume to offer hints, not plans) and in this place, I take the liberty of rementioning the subject, by observing, that a charter is to be understood as a bond of solemn obligation, which the whole enters into, to support the right of every separate part, whether of religion, personal freedom, or property, A firm bargain and a right reckoning make long friends.

In a former page I likewise mentioned the necessity of a large and equal representation; and there is no political matter which more deserves our attention. A small number of electors, or a small number of representatives, are equally dangerous. But if the number of the representatives be not only small, but unequal, the danger is increased. As an instance of this, I mention the following; when the Associators petition was before the House of Assembly of Pennsylvania; twenty-eight members only were present, all the Bucks County members, being eight, voted against it, and had seven of the Chester members done the same, this whole province had been governed by two counties only, and this danger it is always exposed to. The unwarrantable stretch likewise, which that house made in their last sitting, to gain an undue authority over the delegates of that province, ought to warn the people at large, how they trust power out of their own hands. A set of instructions for the Delegates were put together, which in point of sense and business would have dishonored a school-boy, and after being approved by a few, a very few without doors, were carried into the house, and there passed in behalf of the whole colony; whereas, did the whole colony know, with what ill-will that House hath entered on some necessary public measures, they would not hesitate a moment to think them unworthy of such a trust.

Immediate necessity makes many things convenient, which if continued would grow into oppressions. Expedience and right are different things. When the calamities of America required a consultation, there was no method so ready, or at that time so proper, as to appoint persons from the several Houses of Assembly for that purpose and the wisdom with which they have proceeded hath preserved this continent from ruin. But as it is more than probable that we shall never be without a Congress, every well-wisher to good order, must own, that the mode for choosing members of that body, deserves consideration. And I put it as a question to those, who make a study of mankind, whether representation and election is not too great a power for one and the same body of men to possess? When we are planning for posterity, we ought to remember that virtue is not hereditary.

It is from our enemies that we often gain excellent maxims, and are frequently surprised into reason by their mistakes. Mr. Cornwall (one of the Lords of the Treasury) treated the petition of the New York Assembly with contempt, because that House, he said, consisted but of twenty-six members, which trifling number, he argued, could not with decency be put for the whole. We thank him for his involuntary honesty.*

To conclude: However strange it may appear to some, or however unwilling they may be to think so, matters not, but many strong and striking reasons may be given, to show, that nothing can settle our affairs so expeditiously as an open and determined declaration for independence. Some of which are:

First. It is the custom of nations, when any two are at war,

---

* Those who would fully understand of what great consequence a large and equal representation is to a state, should read Burgh's political disquisitions.

for some other powers, not engaged in the quarrel, to step in as mediators, and bring about the preliminaries of a peace: but while America calls herself the subject of Great Britain, no power, however well disposed she may be, can offer her mediation. Wherefore, in our present state we may quarrel on for ever.

Secondly. It is unreasonable to suppose, that France or Spain will give us any kind of assistance, if we mean only to make use of that assistance for the purpose of repairing the breach, and strengthening the connection between Britain and America; because, those powers would be sufferers by the consequences.

Thirdly. While we profess ourselves the subjects of Britain, we must, in the eye of foreign nations, be considered as rebels. The precedent is somewhat dangerous to their peace, for men to be in arms under the name of subjects; we, on the spot, can solve the paradox: but to unite resistance and subjection, requires an idea much too refined for common understanding.

Fourthly. Were a manifesto to be published, and despatched to foreign courts, setting forth the miseries we have endured, and the peaceable methods we have ineffectually used for redress; declaring, at the same time, that not being able, any longer to live happily or safely under the cruel disposition of the British court, we had been driven to the necessity of breaking off all connections with her; at the same time assuring all such courts of our peaceable disposition towards them, and of our desire of entering into trade with them. Such a memorial would produce more good effects to this Continent, than if a ship were freighted with petitions to Britain.

Under our present denomination of British subjects we can neither be received nor heard abroad: The custom of all courts is against us, and will be so, until, by an independance, we take rank with other nations.

These proceedings may at first appear strange and difficult;

but, like all other steps which we have already passed over, will in a little time become familiar and agreeable; and, until an independance is declared, the Continent will feel itself like a man who continues putting off some unpleasant business from day to day, yet knows it must be done, hates to set about it, wishes it over, and is continually haunted with the thoughts of its necessity.

SOURCES

Adams, Guy. " 'Shut Up about Chavez the Killer,' Venezuelan Co-Star Tells Sean Penn." *Independent*, March 8, 2009. http://www.independent.co.uk/news/world/americas/shut-up-about-chavez-the-killer-venezuelan-costar-tells-sean-penn-1639783.html.

Barone, Michael, and Richard E. Cohen. *Almanac of American Politics.* Washington, D.C.: National Journal, 2008. See esp. "CQ Member Profiles" and "Congressional Biographical Directory."

Best, Gary Dean. "The New Deal's War against Economic Recovery: Interview with Gary Dean Best." *Navigator* (July/August, 2000). http://www.objectivistcenter.com/cth—267-The_New_Deals_War_against_Economic_Recovery.aspx.

Block, Sandra. "Rising Costs Make Climb to Higher Education Steeper." *USA Today*, January 12, 2007. http://www.usatoday.com/money/perfi/college/2007-01-12-college-tuition-usat_x.htm.

Brudnick, Ida A. *CRS Report for Congress: Salaries of Members of Congress: A List of Payable Rates and Effective Dates, 1789–2008.* Washington, D.C.: Congressional Research Service, February 21, 2008. http://www.senate.gov/reference/resources/pdf/97-1011.pdf.

Center on Philanthropy at Indiana University. *How Changes in Tax Rates Might Affect Itemized Charitable Deductions.* Indianapolis: Center on Philanthropy at Indiana University, 2009.

Connecticut Office of the Attorney General. *Connecticut Attorney General's Office Press Release: Attorney General Statement On AIG Subpoe-*

nas. Hartford, Conn., March 23, 2009. http://www.ct.gov/ag/cwp/view.asp?A=3673&Q=437228.

Donmoyer, Ryan J. "Rich Donors May Be Undeterred by Tax Caps on Charitable Gifts." *Bloomberg*, March 4, 2009. http://www.bloomberg.com/apps/news?pid=20601103&sid=aRLx2HwnWyWs&refer=us.

Fahrenthold, David A. "House Is Abandoning Carbon Neutral Plan: Move Highlights Congress's Green Struggle." *Washington Post*, March 1, 2009. http://www.washingtonpost.com/wp-dyn/content/article/2009/02/28/AR2009022801947.html?nav=emailpage.

Farley, Robert. "Obama Claims 90 Percent of Guns Recovered in Mexico Come from U.S." *Politifact.com*, April 16, 2009. http://www.politifact.com/truth-o-meter/statements/2009/apr/16/barack-obama/Obama-claims-90-percent-guns-used-Mexico/.

Farrell, Chris. "It's Time to Cure Health Care." *BusinessWeek*, January 23, 2006. http://www.businessweek.com/bwdaily/dnflash/jan2006/nf20060123_1965_db013.htm.

Folsom, Jr., Burton W. *New Deal or Raw Deal? How FDR's Economic Legacy Has Damaged America.* New York: Threshold Editions/Simon & Schuster, 2008.

"Fox News Poll Opinion Dynamics, March 3–4, 2009." *FOXnews.com*, March 5, 2009. http://www.foxnews.com/projects/pdf/030509_Poll.pdf.

"Fox News Poll Opinion Dynamics, March 31–April 1, 2009." *FOXnews.com*, April 2, 2009. http://www.foxnews.com/projects/pdf/040209_FNCPoll.pdf.

GivingUSA Foundation. *GivingUSA Estimates: Key Findings.* Glenview, Ill. GivingUSA, 2008.

Goldberg, Jonah. *Liberal Fascism: The Secret History of the American Left, from Mussolini to the Politics of Change.* New York: Doubleday, 2007.

Goldfarb, Zachary A. "Fannie, Freddie Budget $210 Million On Bonuses, Draw Lawmakers' Fire." *Washington Post*, April 4, 2009. http://www.washingtonpost.com/wp-dyn/content/article/2009/04/03/AR2009040303061.html.

GothamSchools. "Posts tagged 'Mayor Bloomberg.'" *Gothamschools.org*. http://gothamschools.org/tag/mayor-bloomberg/.

Harsanyi, David. "The Freedom to School Your Children at Home." *Denver Post*, March 11, 2008. http://www.denverpost.com/headlines/ci_8524130.

Keating, Christopher. "Democrats Introduce Retroactive Tax Increase." *Hartford Courant*, April 2, 2009. http://www.courant.com/news/politics/hc-dem-budget-plan-0302.0.550902.story.

Kohn, Stephen M. *American Political Prisoners: Prosecutions under the Espionage and Sedition Acts.* Westport, Conn.: Praeger, 1994.

Kurland, Philip B., and Ralph Lerner, eds. *The Founders' Constitution.* See esp. "Chapter 16, Document 15: John Adams, Defense of the Constitutions of Government of the United States." Chicago: University of Chicago Press, 1987.

Lane, Alexander. "Obama Invokes Republican Icons on Health Care." *Politifact.com*, March 5, 2009. http://www.politifact.com/truth-o-meter/statements/2009/mar/05/barack-obama/Obama-goes-back-to-his-Republican-roots-on-health-/.

Maddow, Rachel. "The Rachel Maddow Show for Tuesday, April 7." *Msnbc.com*, April 8, 2009. http://www.msnbc.msn.com/id/30110064/.

Madison, James. *Writings.* New York: Library of America, 1999.

Marx, Karl, and Frederick Engels. *The Communist Manifesto.* Australian National University, 1994. http://www.anu.edu.au/polsci/marx/classics/manifesto.html.

Milloy, Steven. *Green Hell: How Environmentalists Plan to Ruin Your Life and What You Can Do to Stop Them.* Washington, D.C.: Regnery, 2009.

Montopoli, Brian. "Another Obama Nominee Has Tax Issues." *Political Hotsheet* at *CBSNews.com*, March 31, 2009. http://www.cbsnews.com/blogs/2009/03/31/politics/politicalhotsheet/entry4908247.shtml.

Moore, Michael. " 'We the People' to 'King of the World': 'YOU'RE FIRED!' . . . A Letter From Michael Moore." *Michaelmoore.com*, April 1, 2009. http://www.michaelmoore.com/words/message/.

Morrison, Wayne M., and Marc Labonte. *CRS Report for Congress: China's Holdings of U.S. Securities: Implications for the U.S. Economy.* Washington, D.C.: Congressional Research Service, January 9, 2008. http://fpc.state.gov/documents/organization/99496.pdf.

Parents Television Council. "The Alarming Family Hour . . . No Place For Children: A Content Analysis of Sex, Foul Language, and Violence During

Network Television's Family Hour." *Parents Television Council,* September, 2007. http://www.parentstv.org/ptc/publications/reports/familyhour/exsum mary.asp.

Pestritto, Ronald J., and William J. Atto, eds. *American Progressivism: A Reader.* Lanham, Md.: Lexington, 2008.

Public Strategies, Inc. "2009 Public Trust Monitor Opinion Poll Q2," Washington, D.C.: Public Strategies, 2009. http://www.publicstrategiesptm.com.

Rasmussen, Scott. "Most Americans Say Bailouts Were Bad Idea, Political Class Disagrees." *Rasmussen Reports,* April 21, 2009. http://www.rasmussen reports.com/public_content/business/federal_bailout/most_americans_say _bailouts_were_bad_idea_political_class_disagrees.

————."Rasmussen Poll, April 6–7, 2009." *Rasmussen Reports,* April 9, 2009. http://www.rasmussenreports.com/public_content/politics/general_politics/ just_53_say_capitalism_better_than_socialism.

Rehnquist, William H. *All the Laws but One: Civil Liberties in Wartime.* New York: Knopf, 1998.

Rhodehamel, John, comp. *The American Revolution: Writings from the War of Independence.* New York: Library of America, 2001.

Sanner, Ann. "Obama Urges Citizens to Undertake National Service." *Yahoo! News,* April 21, 2009. http://news.yahoo.com/s/ap/20090421/ap_on_go_pr _wh/us_obama_national_service.

Schorn, Daniel. "U.S. Heading For Financial Trouble?" *CBSnews.com,* July 8, 2007. http://www.cbsnews.com/stories/2007/03/01/60minutes/main2528226 _page2.shtml.

Shlaes, Amity. *The Forgotten Man: A New History of the Great Depression.* New York: HarperCollins, 2007.

"Simplifying Tax Systems: The Case for Flat Taxes." *The Economist,* April 16, 2005.

Singer, Peter. "Frequently Asked Questions." *Princeton.edu,* 2009. http:// www.princeton.edu/~psinger/faq.html.

Skousen, W. Cleon. *The 5000-Year Leap: A Miracle That Changed the World.* Malta, Idaho: National Center for Constitutional Studies, 1981.

————. *The Majesty of God's Law.* Salt Lake City, Utah: Ensign, 1996.

Smith, Jean Edward. *FDR*. New York: Random House, 2007.

Sowell, Thomas. *The Housing Boom and Bust*. New York: Basic Books, 2009.

Stossel, John. "Threat to Homeschooling." *Jewish World Review*, April 2, 2008. http://www.jewishworldreview.com/0408/stossel040208.php3.

Swanson, Christopher B. *Cities in Crisis: A Special Analytic Report on High School Graduation*. Bethesda, Md.: Editorial Projects in Education, 2009. http://www.americaspromise.org/uploadedFiles/AmericasPromiseAlliance/Dropout_Crisis/SWANSONCitiesInCrisis040108.pdf.

Tapper, Jake. "Spread the Wealth?" *Political Punch at ABCNews.com*, October 14, 2008. http://blogs.abcnews.com/politicalpunch/2008/10/spread-the-weal.html.

U.S. Bureau of the Census. *The 2000 Statistical Abstract*. See esp. "National Defense Outlays and Veteran Benefits." Washington, D.C., 2000.

U.S. Bureau of the Census. *The 2009 Statistical Abstract*. Washington, D.C., 2009. http://www.census.gov/compendia/statab/.

U.S. Congress. *Budget of the United States Government: Fiscal Year 2009*. Washington, D.C.: February 4, 2009. www.gpoaccess.gov/usbudget/fy09.

U.S. Congress. Congressional Budget Office. *The Budget and Economic Outlook: Fiscal Years 2009–2019*. Washington, D.C., January, 2009. http://www.cbo.gov/doc.cfm?index=9957.

U.S. Department of Commerce. Bureau of Economic Analysis. *National Economic Accounts*. Washington, D.C., 2009.

U.S. Department of Labor. Bureau of Labor Statistics. *Employment Situation Summary*. Washington, D.C., March 2009. http://www.bls.gov/news.release/empsit.nro.htm.

U.S. Department of the Treasury. *Historical Debt Outstanding*. Washington, D.C., 2008. http://www.treasurydirect.gov/govt/reports/pd/histdebt/histdebt.htm.

U.S. Department of the Treasury. Internal Revenue Service. *Selected Expanded Descending Cumulative Percentiles of Returns Based on Income Size Using the Definition of AIG for Each Year, 2001–2006*. Washington, D.C., 2006.

Weil, Martin. "Handgun's Color Leads to Lawsuit." *Washington Post*, March 10, 2009. http://www.washingtonpost.com/wp-dyn/content/article/2009/03/09/AR2009030903240.html.

Williams, Juan. "Obama's Outrageous Sin Against Our Kids." *Fox Forum* at *FOXnews.com*, April 20, 2009. http://foxforum.blogs.foxnews.com/2009/04/20/williams_obama_dc/.

Wilson, Woodrow. *Woodrow Wilson: The Essential Political Writings*. Introduced and Selected by Ronald J. Pestritto. Lanham, Md.: Lexington, 2005.